Early Childhood Interventions

Proven Results, Future Promise

Lynn A. Karoly

M. Rebecca Kilburn, Jill S. Cannon

D0757237

Prepared for
The PNC Financial Services Group, Inc.

 LABOR AND POPULATION

The research described in the report was conducted for The PNC Financial Services Group, Inc. by RAND Labor and Population, a division of the RAND Corporation.

Library of Congress Cataloging-in-Publication Data

Karoly, Lynn A., 1961–
    Early childhood interventions : proven results, future promise / Lynn A. Karoly, M. Rebecca Kilburn, Jill S. Cannon.
      p. cm.
    "MG-341."
    Includes bibliographical references.
    ISBN 0-8330-3836-2 (pbk. : alk. paper)
    1. Children with social disabilities—Services for—United States. 2. Children with social disabilities—Services for—United States—Evaluation. 3. Child welfare—United States—Evaluation. 4. Early childhood education—United States. 5. Child care services—United States. 6. Public welfare—United States. I. Kilburn, M. Rebecca. II. Cannon, Jill S. III. Title.

HV741.K34 2005
362.7'0973—dc22

2005021586

The RAND Corporation is a nonprofit research organization providing objective analysis and effective solutions that address the challenges facing the public and private sectors around the world. RAND's publications do not necessarily reflect the opinions of its research clients and sponsors.

RAND® is a registered trademark.

Cover design by Stephen Bloodsworth

Published 2005 by the RAND Corporation
1776 Main Street, P.O. Box 2138, Santa Monica, CA 90407-2138
1200 South Hayes Street, Arlington, VA 22202-5050
201 North Craig Street, Suite 202, Pittsburgh, PA 15213-1516
RAND URL: http://www.rand.org/
To order RAND documents or to obtain additional information, contact
Distribution Services: Telephone: (310) 451-7002;
Fax: (310) 451-6915; Email: order@rand.org

Preface

In September 2003, The PNC Financial Services Group, Inc. launched *PNC Grow Up Great*, a ten-year, $100-million program to improve school readiness for children from birth to age 5. As part of this initiative, PNC asked the RAND Corporation to prepare a thorough, objective review and synthesis of current research that addresses the potential for interventions of various forms in early childhood to improve outcomes for participating children and their families. In particular, we consider

- the potential consequences of not investing additional resources in the lives of children—particularly disadvantaged children—prior to school entry
- the range of early intervention programs, focusing on those that have been rigorously evaluated
- the demonstrated benefits of interventions with high-quality evaluations and the features associated with successful programs
- the returns to society associated with investing early in the lives of disadvantaged children.

This study was conducted by RAND Labor and Population, building on prior RAND research examining the costs and benefits of early childhood programs. Funding for the project was provided by The PNC Financial Services Group, Inc. The study should be of interest to decisionmakers throughout the United States in the private and public sectors who are considering investing resources in early childhood programs. The findings may also interest practitioners and advocates in the early childhood field.

Contents

Figures

Tables

Summary

Parents, policymakers, business leaders, and the general public increasingly recognize the importance of the first few years in the life of a child for promoting healthy physical, emotional, social, and intellectual development. Nonetheless, many children face deficiencies between ages 0 and 5 in terms of emotional support, intellectual stimulation, or access to resources—due to low income or lack of health care, among other factors—that can impede their ability to develop to their fullest potential. While intervention programs in early childhood are of natural interest to the public sector, the private sector is increasingly playing a role in advocating and effecting increased investments in early childhood.

The *PNC Grow Up Great* initiative is an example of the involvement of the business sector in early childhood investments. This initiative, launched in September 2003 by The PNC Financial Services Group, Inc., is a ten-year, $100-million program to improve school readiness for children from birth to age 5. The PNC initiative encompasses several components, including investing in direct services to disadvantaged children, developing and disseminating information about child development and school readiness through television and print media, promoting employee volunteerism in programs serving children ages 0 to 5, supporting objective research on the costs and benefits of early childhood programs, and advocating for increased access to quality early childhood programs. PNC has partnered with Sesame Workshop, the producers of *Sesame Street*, and Family Communications, Inc., the producers of *Mister Rogers' Neigh-*

borhood, to develop content for the initiative, and the entire effort is guided by a 12-member advisory council of experts in the early childhood field. In the first year of the *PNC Grow Up Great* program, $950,000 in grants has been provided to selected early childhood programs, including Head Start centers and other early childhood education organizations, in PNC's service area (namely Delaware, Indiana, Kentucky, New Jersey, Ohio, and Pennsylvania).

As part of the *PNC Grow Up Great* initiative, PNC asked the RAND Corporation to prepare a thorough, objective review and synthesis of current research that addresses the potential for interventions of various forms in early childhood to improve outcomes for participating children and their families. In particular, as part of this study, we consider

- the potential consequences of not investing additional resources in the lives of children—particularly disadvantaged children—prior to school entry
- the range of early intervention programs, focusing on those that have been rigorously evaluated
- the demonstrated benefits of interventions with high-quality evaluations and the features associated with successful programs
- the returns to society associated with investing early in the lives of disadvantaged children.

Our approach to addressing these questions was to survey the relevant literature, identify the evidence that is scientifically sound, and provide an unbiased perspective on early childhood interventions that can inform decisionmaking on the part of the private and public sectors. Our analysis considers a broad range of interventions implemented throughout the United States, even beyond the types of programs currently supported by the *PNC Grow Up Great* initiative. We here summarize our conclusions.

The period from birth to age 5 is one of opportunity and vulnerability for healthy physical, emotional, social, and cognitive development.

Human development is the result of a complex interplay between genetic endowments and environmental conditions. Both nature and nurture—alone, and in interaction with one another—play key roles throughout the life course. Notably, the first few years of life are a particularly sensitive period in the process of development, laying a foundation for cognitive functioning; behavioral, social, and self-regulatory capacities; and physical health in childhood and beyond. During these early years, a variety of factors are critical to healthy development. They include the nature of early relationships with caregivers, the extent of cognitive stimulation, and access to adequate nutrition and health care. Some children will be resilient in the face of various stressors in early childhood, while healthy development will be compromised for others, with temporary or long-lasting effects.

A sizable fraction of children face risks that may limit their development in the years before school entry.

Risks of developmental delay accrue from living in poverty, having a single parent, and having a mother with less than a high school education, among other factors. Nearly half of a recent cohort of kindergarten children in the United States examined as part of the U.S. Department of Education's Early Childhood Longitudinal Study of the Kindergarten Class of 1998–1999 (ECLS-K) faced at least one of four such risk factors. Nearly one in six was subject to more than one. Exposure to such risks does not necessarily lead to developmental problems. Some children are resilient, but for others, the consequences can be considerable.

Variations in early childhood experiences are manifested in disparities in school readiness, and these gaps often persist.

Disadvantages in early childhood have implications for how prepared children are when they enter school. School readiness includes not only cognitive skills but also those associated with socialization, self-regulatory behavior, and learning approaches. Assessments for the

ECLS-K cohort indicate that children with more-disadvantaged backgrounds enter school with lower levels of the knowledge and social competencies that are important for subsequent school success. While these readiness measures indicate that children from more-enriched environments enter school better prepared, longitudinal data demonstrate that these early gaps persist and even widen as children progress through school. Thus, because disadvantaged children do not advance at the same rate at their more advantaged peers, achievement gaps tend to widen over time. Children from disadvantaged backgrounds also experience higher rates of special education use, grade repetition, and dropping out of high school. Lower rates of school achievement are in turn associated with unfavorable trajectories in later years. The latter include such outcomes as low rates of employment, welfare dependency, and delinquency and crime. Even if only a portion of these detrimental outcomes in childhood and adulthood can be averted, the benefits may be substantial.

Early childhood interventions are designed to counteract various stressors in early childhood and promote healthy development.

Early childhood interventions are designed to provide a protective influence to compensate for the various risk factors that potentially compromise healthy child development in the years before school entry. While they share a common objective, early childhood interventions are highly varied in their methods; there is no uniform model. Programs vary in the outcomes they aim to improve and in the risk factors they consider for eligibility to participate, e.g., low socioeconomic status, single parenthood. They differ in whether they target the child, the parent, or both, and in the extent of individualized attention they provide. Different programs target children of different ages and vary in what kind of services they provide, where they provide them, and for how many hours per week.

Rigorous evaluations of early childhood interventions can help us understand what outcomes they may improve.

Although we may expect early childhood programs to produce beneficial effects, a scientifically sound evaluation is required to know whether they fulfill their promise. The variation in early childhood intervention approaches suggests that such evaluations are needed for the full range of program models, ideally with the ability to ascertain the effects of varying key program features.

The best evaluation designs are those that provide the highest confidence that effects attributed to the program are indeed the result of the intervention, rather than some other influential factor or factors. Randomized experiments are ideal, but such designs are not always feasible, so carefully designed and implemented quasi-experimental methods may suffice as an alternative.

While many early childhood interventions have been implemented, and a subset of those have been evaluated in some fashion, only a relatively small subset have been evaluated using scientifically sound methods. After reviewing the literature on studies of early childhood interventions that met our criteria for rigorous evaluation, we identified published evaluations for 20 early childhood programs with well-implemented experimental designs or strong quasi-experimental designs (see Table S.1 for a list of the programs grouped according to the types of services provided). In selecting these 20, we excluded some programs because their evaluations did not meet minimum standards for scientific rigor (e.g., a large enough sample size). Sixteen programs had the strongest evidence base in that they measure outcomes at the time of kindergarten entry or beyond. The remaining four programs are labeled as having a promising evidence base because, as of the last follow-up, many or all of the children were as young as age 2 or 3, so there is less information as to the effect of the program on outcomes when the children are closer to the age of school entry or once the children have entered school.

Scientific research has demonstrated that early childhood interventions can improve the lives of participating children and families.

We examined the following benefit domains: cognition and academic achievement, behavioral and emotional competencies, educational progression and attainment, child maltreatment, health, delinquency and crime, social welfare program use, and labor market success. For

Table S.1
Early Childhood Intervention Programs Included in Study

Home Visiting or Parent Education
Nurse-Family Partnership (NFP)
Developmentally Supportive Care: Newborn Individualized Developmental Care and Assessment Program (DSC/NIDCAP)*
Parents as Teachers*
Project CARE (Carolina Approach to Responsive Education)—no early childhood education
HIPPY (Home Instruction Program for Preschool Youngsters) USA
Reach Out and Read*
DARE to be You
Incredible Years

Home Visiting or Parent Education Combined with Early Childhood Education
Early Head Start*
Syracuse Family Development Research Program (FDRP)
Comprehensive Child Development Program (CCDP)
Infant Health and Development Program (IHDP)
Project CARE (Carolina Approach to Responsive Education)—with early childhood education
Carolina Abecedarian Project
Houston Parent-Child Development Center (PCDC)
Early Training Project (ETP)
High/Scope Perry Preschool Project
Chicago Child-Parent Centers (CPC)
Head Start

Early Childhood Education Only
Oklahoma Pre-K

NOTES: Programs marked with an asterisk are designated as having a *promising* evidence base because a substantial number of children were as young as age 2 or 3 at the time of the last follow-up. All other programs are designated as having a *strong* evidence base.

each of these domains (with the exception of social welfare program use), statistically significant benefits were found in at least two-thirds of the programs we reviewed that measured outcomes in that domain (see Tables S.2 and S.3). In some cases, the improved outcomes in these domains were demonstrated soon after the program ended, while in other cases the favorable effects were observed through adolescence and in the transition to adulthood. In one case, lasting benefits were measured 35 years after the intervention ended. Even though there is evidence that early benefits in terms of cognition or school achievement may eventually fade, the evidence indicates that there can be longer-lasting gains in educational progress and attainment, labor market outcomes, dependency, and pro-social behaviors. A few studies also indicate that the parents of participating children can also benefit from early intervention programs, particularly when they are specifically targeted by the intervention.

The magnitudes of the favorable effects can often be sizable. The size of the effects tend to be more modest for cognitive and behavioral measures, and, as noted, the favorable gains in these measures often shrink in size over time. The effects are more substantial and long-lasting for outcomes such as special education placement and grade retention, as well as some of the other outcomes in adolescence and adulthood. At the same time, it is important to note that the improved outcomes realized by participants in targeted early intervention programs are typically not large enough to fully compensate for the disadvantages those children face. Thus, while early intervention programs can improve outcomes over what they otherwise would have been, they typically do not fully close the gap between the disadvantaged children they serve and their more advantaged peers.

While the evidence from the programs we review is compelling, it is important to note that these programs do not represent all early childhood programs or even the subset of effective programs. Moreover, evidence of the effectiveness of a given program does not imply that all similar programs will have the same effect or even that

Table S.2
Measured Outcomes and Program Effects for Early Childhood Intervention Evaluations—Child Outcomes

Program	Domain					
	Cognitive/ Achievement	Behavioral/ Emotional	Educational	Child Maltreatment	Health, Accidents, and Injuries	Crime
Home Visiting or Parent Education						
NFP	Achievement test scores	Positive behaviors		Child abuse	Emergency room visits Hospital days	Arrests
DSC/ NIDCAP[a]	Mental indices	Developmental delay			Reflexes Weight gain Hospital stays	
Parents as Teachers[a]	Achievement test scores	Positive behaviors		Child maltreatment	Child health rating Injuries	
Project CARE (no ECE)	//////					
HIPPY USA	Achievement test scores					
Reach Out and Read[a]	Vocabulary					
DARE to be You	Developmental level	Behavior problems				
Incredible Years		Behavior problems Social competence				
Home Visiting or Parent Education Combined with Early Childhood Education						
Early Head Start[a]	Achievement test scores	Positive behaviors			Child health rating	
Syracuse FDRP	IQ	Positive behaviors	Grades (girls) Attendance (girls) Teacher ratings (girls)			
CCDP	//////	//////	//////			
IHDP	IQ Achievement test scores	Behavior problems	//////		//////	
Project CARE (with ECE)	IQ					
Abecedarian	IQ Achievement test scores		Special education Grade retention			

Table S.2—continued

Program	Domain					
	Cognitive/ Achievement	Behavioral/ Emotional	Educational	Child Maltreatment	Health, Accidents, and Injuries	Crime
Home Visiting or Parent Education Combined with Early Childhood Education (continued)						
Houston PCDC	IQ Achievement test scores	Behavior problems				
ETP	IQ Achievement test scores		Special education		Teen pregnancy	
Perry Preschool	IQ Achievement test scores		Special education		Teen pregnancy	Arrests
Chicago CPC	Achievement test scores	Social competence	Special education Grade retention	Child abuse		Delinquency
Head Start	IQ Achievement test scores (mixed)		Grade retention		Immunizations Other positive health behaviors	
Early Childhood Education Only						
Oklahoma Pre-K	Achievement test scores					

☐ Outcome measured and improvement in the listed indicator was statistically significant at the 0.05 level or better.

▧ Outcome measured but difference was not statistically significant at the 0.05 level or better.

▨ Outcome not measured.

SOURCE: Table 3.1.

NOTES: See Table S.1 for full program names and Table 2.3 for program implementation dates and sample sizes.

[a] At the last follow-up, these programs measured outcomes for children as young as age 2 or 3.

RAND MG341-T-S.2b

Table S.3
Measured Outcomes and Program Effects for Early Childhood Intervention Evaluations—Adult Outcomes

Program	Adult Outcome Domain			
	Educational Attainment	Employment and Earnings	Social Services Use	Crime
Home Visiting or Parent Education Combined with Early Childhood Education				
Abecedarian	Years of completed schooling Ever attended four-year college	Skilled employment	////	////
ETP	////			
Perry Preschool	High school graduation	Employment Earnings Income	Use of social services	Arrests Arrests for violent crimes Time in prison/jail
Chicago CPC	High school graduation Highest grade completed			Arrests Arrests for violent crimes
Head Start	High school graduation (whites) College attendance (whites)	////		Booked or charged with crime (blacks)

☐ Outcome measured and improvement in the listed indicator was statistically significant at the 0.05 level or better.

▨ Outcome measured but difference was not statistically significant at the 0.05 level or better.

▉ Outcome not measured.

SOURCE: Table 3.2.

NOTES: See Table S.1 for full program names and Table 2.3 for program implementation dates and sample sizes.

RAND *MG341-T-S.3*

the same program implemented under different conditions will have the same effects. Ultimately, program effects may vary because of a variety of factors, including program design, the population served, and the local context in which a program is delivered.

A very limited evidence base points to several program features that may be associated with better outcomes for children: better-trained caregivers, smaller child-to-staff ratios, and greater intensity of services.

Based on experimental and quasi-experimental evaluations of program design features, as well as comparisons of effects across model programs, three features appear to be associated with more-effective interventions. First, programs with better-trained caregivers appear to be more effective. In the context of center-based programs, this may take the form of a lead teacher with a college degree as opposed to no degree. In the context of home visiting programs, researchers have found stronger effects when services are provided by a trained nurse as opposed to a paraprofessional or lay professional home visitor. Second, in the context of center-based programs, there is evidence to suggest that programs are more successful when they have smaller child-to-staff ratios. Third, there is some evidence that more-intensive programs are associated with better outcomes, but not enough to indicate the optimal number of program hours and how they might vary with child risk characteristics. One might expect that some minimum level of program hours is required for there to be any benefit but that, as hours increase, returns increase at a diminishing rate. It is noteworthy that the features associated with more-successful programs are costly. Thus, it appears that more money may need to be spent to obtain larger effects—at least up to a point.

The favorable effects of early childhood programs can translate into dollar benefits for the government, participants, and other members of society.

Early childhood interventions may range in cost from modest to a considerable financial investment. It is therefore reasonable to ask whether the costs can be justified in terms of the benefits associated with the programs. Many of those benefits can be translated into dollar figures. For example, if school outcomes improve, fewer resources may be spent on remedial education services in the form of repeated grades or special education classes. If improvements in school performance lead to higher educational attainment and subsequent economic success in adulthood, the government may benefit from higher tax revenues and reduced outlays for social welfare programs and the criminal justice system. As a result of improved economic outcomes, participants themselves benefit from higher lifetime incomes, while other members of society gain from reduced levels of delinquency and crime. It should be kept in mind, however, that some of the improved outcomes associated with early childhood interventions cannot be readily translated into dollar benefits. That is the case, for example, for cognitive development and behavioral improvements.

Economic analyses of several early childhood interventions demonstrate that effective programs can repay the initial investment with savings to government and benefits to society down the road.

One or more benefit-cost analyses have been conducted for seven of the 20 programs we studied. In addition, benefit-cost meta-analyses have been conducted for home visiting programs serving at-risk children and for early childhood education programs serving low-income three- and four-year-olds. These studies employ accepted methods for benefit-cost analysis based on the associated rigorous outcome evaluations. The results for these benefit-cost studies are summarized in Table S.4, with columns showing present-value costs and present-value benefits to society per child served, along with net benefits per child, and the benefit-cost ratio. In recognition of the differing follow-up periods (shown in the second column), the results are presented in four panels based on the age of participants at the time of the last follow-up: the elementary school years, the secondary school years, early adulthood, and middle adulthood.

Because of differences in methodology—such as which benefits were measured and monetized, the length of the follow-up period, and the projection of future benefits beyond the last age of follow-up—the benefit-cost results in Table S.4 are not strictly comparable across early childhood interventions. Thus, while these results cannot identify which programs have the "biggest bang for the buck," they can demonstrate whether, in principle, early childhood intervention programs can generate benefits that outweigh the program costs.

One of the seven individual programs evaluated (the Comprehensive Child Development Program, or CCDP) was not shown to be effective, so it could not generate net economic benefits. A second program (the Infant Health and Development Program, or IHDP) had favorable effects as of the last follow-up at age 8, but the outcomes assessed could not be translated into dollar savings. For the remaining studies (including the meta-analyses), the estimates of net benefits per child served range from about $1,400 per child to nearly $240,000 per child (see Table S.4). Viewed another way, the returns to society for each dollar invested extend from $1.26 to $17.07. Positive net benefits were found for programs that required a large investment (over $40,000 per child), as well as those that cost considerably less (under $2,000 per child). Programs with per-child costs in the middle of this range also generated positive net benefits. The economic returns were favorable for programs that focused on home visiting or parent education, as well as those that combined those services with early childhood education.

The largest benefit-cost ratios were associated with programs with longer-term follow-up (i.e., moving farther down Table S.4), because they allowed measurement at older ages of outcomes such as educational attainment, delinquency and crime, earnings, and other outcomes that most readily translate into dollar benefits. Not only do the studies with measured improvements based on long-term follow-up demonstrate that the benefits from early interventions can be long-lasting, they also give more confidence that the savings the programs generate can be substantial. Programs with evaluations that have followed children only until school entry or a few years beyond typically do not measure those outcomes that are likely to be associated with the largest dollar benefits, although they may eventually generate large savings as well.

Because not all benefits from the interventions could be translated into dollar values, our benefit-cost estimates for effective programs are likely to be conservative. Moreover, such analyses do not incorporate some of the other benefits from effective early interventions. These could include improved labor market performance for

Table S.4
Benefit-Cost Results for Selected Early Childhood Intervention Programs

Program	Type	Age at Last Follow-Up	Program Costs per Child ($)	Total Benefits to Society per Child ($)	Net Benefits to Society per Child ($)	Benefit-Cost Ratio
Follow-Up During Elementary School Years						
CCDP	Combo	5	37,388	−9	−37,397	—
HIPPY USA	HV/PE	6	1,681	3,032	1,351	1.80
IHDP	Combo	8	49,021	0	−49,021	—
Follow-Up During Secondary School Years						
NFP—higher-risk sample	HV/PE	15	7,271	41,419	34,148	5.70
NFP—lower-risk sample	HV/PE	15	7,271	9,151	1,880	1.26
NFP—full sample	HV/PE	15	9,118	26,298	17,180	2.88
HV for at-risk mothers and children (meta-analysis)	HV/PE	Varies	4,892	10,969	6,077	2.24

Table S.4—continued

Program	Type	Age at Last Follow-Up	Program Costs per Child ($)	Total Benefits to Society per Child ($)	Net Benefits to Society per Child ($)	Benefit-Cost Ratio
Follow-Up to Early Adulthood						
Abecedarian	Combo	21	42,871	138,635	95,764	3.23
Chicago CPC	Combo	21	6,913	49,337	42,424	7.14
Perry Preschool (excluding intangible crime costs)	Combo	27	14,830	76,426	61,595	5.15
Perry Preschool (including intangible crime costs)	Combo	27	14,830	129,622	114,792	8.74
ECE for low-income three- and four-year-olds (meta-analysis)	Combo	Varies	6,681	15,742	9,061	2.36
Follow-Up to Middle Adulthood						
Perry Preschool	Combo	40	14,830	253,154	238,324	17.07

SOURCE: Table 4.4.

NOTES: See Table S.2 for full program names and Table 2.3 for program implementation dates and sample sizes. All dollar values are 2003 dollars per child and are the present value of amounts over time where future values are discounted to age 0 of the participating child, using a 3 percent annual real discount rate. Numbers may not sum due to rounding; n.a. = not available; Combo = HV/parent education combined with ECE; ECE = early childhood education; HV = home visiting; PE = parent education.

the parents of participating children, as well as stronger national economic competitiveness as a result of improvements in educational attainment of the future workforce.

The economic benefits of early childhood interventions are likely to be greater for programs that effectively serve targeted, disadvantaged children than for programs that serve lower-risk children.
There is some evidence that the economic returns from investing in early intervention programs are larger when programs are effectively targeted. In the Nurse-Family Partnership home visiting program, the effects were larger for a higher-risk sample of mothers (see Table S.4). Consequently, the return for each dollar invested was $5.70 for the higher-risk population served but only $1.26 for the lower-risk population. This finding indicates that it is not reasonable to expect the returns we report for specific programs serving specific disadvantaged populations to apply when the same program serves a different population. In particular, we would not expect to see the same returns in a universal program, e.g., a state-run preschool program open to all, although net benefits from such universal programs may still be positive and the associated benefit-cost ratios may still exceed 1.

It is important to acknowledge that our conclusions rest on a solid, but still limited, evidence base. And that evidence base can always be strengthened by further research and evaluation of early childhood intervention programs. Nevertheless, for decisionmakers considering investments in early childhood interventions, our findings indicate that a body of sound research exists that can guide resource allocation decisions. This evidence base sheds light on the types of programs that have been demonstrated to be effective, the features associated with effective programs, and the potential for returns to society that exceed the resources invested in program delivery. These proven results signal the future promise of investing early in the lives of disadvantaged children.

Acknowledgments

We wish to thank the sponsors of this research, The PNC Financial Services Group, Inc. In particular, we thank Eva Blum, Sally McCrady, and James Rohr, who provided the motivation for this effort and information about the *PNC Grow Up Great* initiative. We also benefited from the feedback provided by members of the *PNC Grow Up Great* Advisory Council.

Among our RAND colleagues, we are grateful for the research assistance provided by Florencia Jaureguiberry, Arnab Mukherji, and Jennifer Wong. We are indebted to Michael Stoto for generous statistical advice, including the use of specialized meta-analysis software that enhanced the quantitative analysis. James Chiesa provided valuable editorial assistance and wrote the summary, and Miriam Polon's editing of the manuscript further improved our prose. We also appreciate the administrative assistance of Ruth Eagle-Winsick and Mechelle Wilkins. The RAND Labor and Population review process employs anonymous peer reviewers, including at least one reviewer who is external to the RAND Corporation. In our case, the technical reviews of the two anonymous reviewers greatly improved the exposition and empirical components of the study.

Abbreviations

CARE	(Project) Carolina Approach to Responsive Education
CCDP	Comprehensive Child Development Program
CED	Committee for Economic Development
CPC	(Chicago) Child-Parent Centers (program)
CPI-U	Consumer Price Index for All Urban Consumers
DSC	Developmentally Supportive Care (NIDCAP)
ECE	early childhood education
ECLS-K	Early Childhood Longitudinal Study—Kindergarten Class of 1998–1999
ETP	Early Training Project
FDRP	(Syracuse) Family Development Research Program
GED	General Educational Development test (high school equivalency)
HIPPY	Home Instruction Program for Preschool Youngsters
HV	home visiting
IHDP	Infant Health and Development Program
IRR	internal rate of return
NAEP	National Assessment of Educational Progress
NFP	Nurse-Family Partnership (program)
NIDCAP	Newborn Individualized Developmental Care and Assessment Program

PCDC   (Houston) Parent-Child Development Center
PEIP   Prenatal/Early Infancy Project
SES   socioeconomic status

CHAPTER ONE

Introduction

Parents, policymakers, business leaders, and the general public increasingly recognize the importance of the first few years in the life of a child for promoting healthy physical, emotional, social, and intellectual development. Whether the evidence comes from sophisticated research by brain scientists or the simple observation of the developmental milestones of an infant, toddler, or preschooler, it is clear that the years prior to kindergarten entry represent a foundational period for ensuring children's eventual success in school and beyond. An explosion of recent research contributes to our understanding of the complex and dynamic ways that both nature and nurture—genetics and the environment—operate together to shape the developing brain and the resulting emotional, social, regulatory, moral, and intellectual capacities that emerge (Shonkoff and Phillips, 2000).

Nonetheless, many children face deficiencies between ages 0 and 5 in terms of emotional support, intellectual stimulation, or access to resources—because of low income or lack of health care among other factors—that can impede their ability to develop to their fullest potential. Early childhood interventions—ranging from home visiting programs in the first few years of life to high-quality center-based preschool education in the year or two before kindergarten entry—have been created to counteract these stressors and provide young children and their families with needed supports. The enthusiasm on the part of the public and policymakers for such programs has led many states and localities to devote increasing resources to early childhood initiatives, especially those that have a proven record of improving children's outcomes. These new efforts complement spending by the federal government in support of disadvantaged families with young children through programs that provide direct services, such as Early Head Start and Head Start, along with those that provide cash assistance and other resources through means-tested social welfare programs.

While intervention programs in early childhood are of natural interest to parents and the public sector, the private sector is increasingly playing a role in advocating increased investments in early childhood. The involvement stems in part from the recognition that the quality of the future labor force, as well as the base of future consumers, depends upon the success of cohorts that are being born today. Businesses recognize the economic investment value of early childhood programs. For example, in 2002, the Committee for Economic Development (CED), an influential group of more than 250 leaders in the business and education communities, released an analysis that endorsed universal access to high-quality preschool programs for children ages 3 and 4 (CED, 2002). This support was echoed in a report issued a year later by two other prominent groups of business leaders—the Business Roundtable and Corporate Voices for Working America—which recommended expanding early childhood programs for children ages 3 and 4 (Business Roundtable and Corporate Voices for Working Families, 2003). A number of private foundations also have initiatives promoting early childhood programs, including the Preschool for All initiative of the Packard Foundation and the support for preschool education by the Pew Charitable Trusts.[1]

In other cases, high-profile leaders in the community have led the call to invest in early childhood programs. Rob Reiner and his "I Am Your Child" campaign played a key role in the passage of Proposition 10 in California (the California Children and Families Act of 1998), now called the First 5 California initiative.[2] The First 5

---

[1] For descriptions of these initiatives by Packard and Pew, see http://www.packard.org/index.cgi?page=cfc-upe and http://www.pewtrusts.com/ideas/index.cfm?issue=26, respectively.

[2] See http://www.ccfc.ca.gov.

program, implemented within California's 58 counties, provides a range of programs for families with children from birth to school entry with funding from a dedicated sales tax on cigarettes. In 2002, David Lawrence, Jr., retired publisher of *The Miami Herald*, was a major force behind a Florida ballot initiative that approved a constitutional amendment requiring the state to provide voluntary, high-quality preschool for all Florida four-year-olds.[3]

The *PNC Grow Up Great* initiative is an example of the involvement of the business sector in early childhood investments. This initiative, launched in September 2003 by PNC Financial Services Group, Inc., is a ten-year, $100-million program to improve school readiness for children from birth to age 5.[4] The PNC initiative encompasses several components: investing in direct services to disadvantaged children, developing and disseminating information about child development and school readiness through television and print media, promoting employee volunteerism in programs serving children ages 0–5, supporting objective research on the costs and benefits of early childhood programs, and advocating for increased access to quality early childhood programs.

In the first year of the *PNC Grow Up Great* program, $950,000 in grants has been provided to selected early childhood programs, including 11 Head Start centers as well as other early childhood education organizations, in the bank's service area (namely Delaware, Indiana, Kentucky, New Jersey, Ohio, and Pennsylvania). *PNC Grow Up Great* has partnered with Sesame Workshop, the producers of *Sesame Street*, and Family Communications, Inc., the producers of *Mister Rogers' Neighborhood*, to underwrite new television programming for preschoolers and distribute school readiness kits to families with young children. Public service announcements, Internet content, and ads in print and other outlets highlight the importance of early childhood opportunities for children, with messages designed to reach parents and caregivers, as well as general audiences in the public and pri-

---

[3] For details on the Florida program, see http://www.upkflorida.org.

[4] For further information on the initiative, see http://www.pncgrowupgreat.com.

vate sectors. An online system has been developed to allow PNC's 24,000 employees to identify volunteer opportunities with early childhood programs, with the bank providing relevant training and other supports.[5] In addition, PNC has supported research and other outreach activities to raise awareness of the need for and benefits from access to high-quality early childhood programs and the opportunities for supporting such programs through the public and private sectors. A 12-member advisory council of experts in the field of early childhood provides critical guidance for the initiative.

As part of the *PNC Grow Up Great* initiative, PNC asked the RAND Corporation to prepare a thorough, objective review and synthesis of current research that addresses the potential for interventions of various forms in early childhood to improve outcomes for participating children and their families. In particular, as part of this study, we consider

- the potential consequences of not investing additional resources in the lives of children—particularly disadvantaged children— prior to school entry
- the range of early intervention programs, focusing on those that have been rigorously evaluated
- the demonstrated benefits of interventions with high-quality evaluations and the features associated with successful programs
- the returns to society associated with investing early in the lives of disadvantaged children.

Our approach to addressing these questions is to survey the relevant literature, identify the evidence that is scientifically sound, and provide an unbiased perspective on early childhood interventions that can inform decisionmaking on the part of the private and public sectors. Our analysis considers a broad range of interventions implemented throughout the United States, even beyond the types of programs currently supported by the *PNC Grow Up Great* initiative.

---

[5] PNC covers up to 40 hours of paid time off per year for such volunteer activities.

Our analysis builds on a prior RAND study, *Investing in Our Children: What We Know and Don't Know About the Costs and Benefits of Early Childhood Interventions* (Karoly et al., 1998), which provided a synthesis of ten early childhood intervention programs. In that study, we focused on the associated benefits for participating children and families that had been demonstrated through rigorous program evaluation. For two of the ten programs, we were also able to compare the costs of the program with the dollar value of the resulting benefits. As part of this study, we again draw on the research literature to update the list of programs we considered in *Investing in Our Children*. Based on new research that has emerged since our last synthesis, we examine a larger group of programs, both for the synthesis of program benefits and for the review of the economic returns associated with such programs.

Like RAND's earlier study, our analysis focuses on early childhood interventions that provide services to at-risk children and/or their families at some time during the period of early childhood—as early as the prenatal period or as late as the year or two prior to kindergarten entry. We limit ourselves to programs that aim to improve child cognitive or socioemotional development, perhaps as one of several objectives, and that have been implemented and evaluated in the United States since 1960. We do not cover programs that are designed primarily to promote children's physical health, nor do we cover programs that primarily serve children with special needs.

To motivate our focus on early childhood interventions, in the remainder of this chapter, we call attention to the disparities in opportunities and outcomes in early childhood and the associated consequences for school performance and success in adulthood. This discussion highlights potential opportunities to intervene early in the lives of disadvantaged children to promote healthier physical, social, emotional, and cognitive development. The final section outlines the issues we address in the remaining chapters and provides a road map for the rest of the report.

Disparities in Early Childhood and the Associated Consequences

While most children in the years before school entry experience a supportive home and neighborhood environment and have access to sufficient financial and nonfinancial resources to support healthy development and school readiness, many other children are not so fortunate. Numerous indicators highlight the substantial differences in early childhood experiences across children, differences that affect their initial school readiness, differences that persist as children age. Recent data from various sources illustrate some of these patterns of early disadvantage:

- *Low birthweight affects a small but growing fraction of newborns.* In 2003, 8 percent of births were classified as low birthweight (less than 2,500 grams), the highest fraction since the early 1970s. Black non-Hispanic babies are twice as likely to be low birthweight as their white non-Hispanic counterparts (13.5 percent versus 7.0 percent). Low-birthweight babies are at risk of delayed motor and social development, and poor school achievement.[6]
- *Preventive health care does not reach all young children.* As of 2002, 12 percent of children under age 2 had not had a well-child checkup in the past year. That fraction rises to 16 percent among children ages 2 to 3 and to 18 percent for children ages 4 to 5. Children who do not receive these checkups miss an opportunity for health care providers to conduct developmental screenings and to encourage parental behaviors that promote healthy child development.[7]
- *Poverty in early childhood affects a sizable share of young children.* The latest data from 2003 indicate that 20 percent of children

---

[6] Data are from the National Center for Health Statistics as reported in Child Trends (2003).

[7] Data are from the National Health Interview Survey. See Child Trends and Center for Health Research (2004), Chart 6-1.

under age 6 (4.7 million children) live in families with income below the poverty line ($18,660 for a family of four). The poverty rate is 53 percent among children under age 6 living in female-headed households, 39 percent for African-American children, and 32 percent for Latino children. Poverty has been shown to be particularly detrimental in early childhood in terms of children's subsequent educational and other life-course outcomes (Haveman and Wolfe, 1995; Mayer, 1997; Duncan and Brooks-Gunn, 1997).[8]

- *Neighborhood environments do not support healthy development for many young children.* Data from the 2000 Census reveal that 22 percent of children under age 5 lived in neighborhoods where 20 percent or more of the population had income below the poverty line. These neighborhoods of concentrated poverty provide more limited opportunities in terms of social interaction, positive role models, and other resources important for early child development (e.g., quality child care, health facilities, parks and playgrounds).[9]

- *Early literacy at home lags for some young children.* Within families of three- to five-year-olds, 16 percent are not read to regularly (three or more times a week), and 26 percent are not regularly taught letters, words, or numbers. Just under half are frequently told a story or taught songs or music. The differential in reading is particularly striking by the level of mother's education: 31 percent of children whose mothers have less than a high school education are not read to regularly compared with 7 percent of those whose mothers have a college degree. These are all early literacy-building activities associated with better school performance in kindergarten and beyond (Snow, Burns, and

---

[8] Data are from the 2004 Current Population Survey. See Child Trends and Center for Child Health Research (2004), Charts 9-3 and 9-4.

[9] See Child Trends and Center for Child Health Research (2004), Chart 7-1.

Griffin, 1998; Burgess, Hecht, and Lonigan, 2002; U.S. Department of Education, 2003).[10]

These early indicators of disadvantage have implications for how prepared children are when they first enter school at kindergarten. While there is no single definition of school readiness, experts agree that readiness is a multifaceted concept that goes beyond academic and cognitive skills to include physical, social, and emotional development, as well as approaches to learning (Vandivere et al., 2004). A series of assessments for a recent kindergarten cohort, examined as part of the U.S. Department of Education's nationally representative Early Childhood Longitudinal Study of the Kindergarten Class of 1998–1999 (ECLS-K), indicate that disadvantaged children enter school lagging their more advantaged peers in terms of the knowledge and social competencies that are widely recognized as enabling children to perform at even the most basic level (West, Denton, and Germino-Hausken, 2000).

Table 1.1 shows the fraction of children with skills at various levels in print familiarity, reading, and mathematics at kindergarten entry, in total and for subgroups defined by mother's education, family type, welfare receipt (an indicator of poverty status), and the primary language spoken at home. For each measure, disadvantaged children—those whose mothers have less education, who live in single-parent families, whose families have received welfare, and who do not speak English at home—are less likely to demonstrate the indicated skill. For example, whereas 18 percent of children overall are not familiar with basic conventions of print or writing (e.g., knowing that English is read from left to right and top to bottom, or where a story ends), that fraction is 32 percent for children whose mothers have less than a high school education but only 8 percent for children whose mothers have a college degree or higher. Similar patterns hold for the other indicators of at-risk status. Substantial gaps are also evi-

---

[10] Data are for 2001 and based on the National Household Education Survey. See U.S. Department of Education (2003), Table 37-1.

Table 1.1
Measures of School Readiness at Kindergarten Entry by Family Characteristics (percentage)

	Print Familiarity	Reading Proficiency Level		Mathematics Proficiency Level	
	0 Skills[a]	First[b]	Second[c]	Second[d]	Third[e]
Total	18	66	29	58	20
Mother's education					
Less than high school	32	38	9	32	6
High school diploma or equivalent	23	57	20	50	13
Some college	17	69	30	61	20
Bachelor's degree or higher	8	86	50	79	37
Family type					
Single mother	26	53	18	44	11
Single father	22	58	21	51	16
Without parent	16	70	33	63	23
Welfare receipt					
Utilized AFDC	32	41	11	33	6
Never utilized AFDC	17	69	31	61	22
Primary language spoken at home					
Not English	26	49	20	45	13
English	18	67	30	59	21

SOURCE: West, Denton, and Germino-Hausken (2000), Tables 5, 6 and 7.

NOTES: Estimates are based on first-time kindergarten children assessed in English. Approximately 19 percent of Asian children and 30 percent of Hispanic children were not assessed.

[a] Print familiarity measures three items: knowing that English is read from left to right, is read from bottom to top, and where a reading passage ends. Those with no skills are not familiar with any of these concepts.

[b] The first reading proficiency level measures recognition of upper and lower case letters of the alphabet.

[c] The second reading proficiency level measures phonological sensitivity at the subword level, in this case knowledge of letter and sound relationships at the beginning of words.

[d] The second mathematics proficiency level measures reading numerals, counting beyond 10, sequencing patterns, and using nonstandard units of length to compare objects.

[e] The third mathematics proficiency level measures number sequence, reading two-digit numerals, identification of the ordinal position of an object, and solving a word problem.

dent in measures of reading and mathematics proficiency.[11] On most of these indicators, one of the sharpest contrasts from least-prepared to most-prepared is for children differentiated by mother's education level.

The ECLS-K also assessed pro-social behaviors, behavior problems, and readiness to learn at kindergarten entry, based on responses from both parents and teachers. While the majority of children exhibit positive behaviors such as forming friendships with classmates, and only a small minority are rated as having behavior problems such as fighting or arguing with others or getting mad easily, disadvantaged children are less likely to exhibit the positive behaviors and more likely to exhibit the problem ones, according to both parental and teacher reports. Similar patterns are evident for other outcomes, including fine and gross motor skills, measures of physical health, and developmental difficulties (West, Denton, and Germino-Hausken, 2000).

These measures of school readiness suggest that children from more-enriched environments enter school better prepared. The longitudinal data from the ECLS-K and other data assessed by Heckman and Masterov (2004) demonstrate that these early differences expand as children progress through school. In other words, because disadvantaged children do not progress at the same rate as their more advantaged peers, the achievement gap tends to widen over time. For the ECLS-K cohort, children with two or more family risk factors (mother's education less than high school, single parent, income below the poverty line, and primary home language other than English) began with lower reading and mathematics achievement scores at kindergarten entry. By third grade, the at-risk children had gained 73 points, on average, in reading achievement compared with 84 points for children with none of the risk factors, thereby expanding the

---

[11] For mathematics proficiency, Table 1.1 records results starting at the second proficiency level because 94 percent of children attain the first proficiency level (measuring reading numerals, recognizing shapes, and counting to 10). See West, Denton, and Germino-Hausken (2000), Table 7.

achievement gap. The differential in math gains was 57 points versus 65 points. Using income to measure the level of advantage, Heckman and Masterov (2004) use longitudinal data from the National Longitudinal Survey of Youth to demonstrate that the percentile ranks on math achievement scores for children from the lowest income quartile and those from the highest income quartile widen between ages 6 and 12.[12] They also find a more modest growth in the gap across income quartiles in the percentile rank for an antisocial behavior score.

The achievement gaps are also evident in national educational assessments of student performance in terms of basic proficiency in core subjects. On average, 26 percent of 8th graders in 2003 scored below the "basic" level of achievement in reading on the National Assessment of Educational Progress (NAEP), indicating they do not have even partial mastery of the knowledge and skills "fundamental for proficient work" at that grade level. For children whose parents have less than a high school education, the fraction scoring below the basic achievement level was 45 percent, 26 percentage points higher than that of their peers whose parents have graduated from college (for whom 19 percent score below basic achievement) (U.S. Department of Education, 2004b).[13] The gap in mathematics proficiency at the same grade level is even higher: Thirty-three percentage points separate the students with the least-educated parents from those with the most-educated (56 percent below the basic achievement level for students whose parents have less than a high school education versus 23 percent whose parents are college graduates) (U.S. Department of Education, 2004a).[14] These gaps are similar when students are com-

---

[12] Each income quartile captures 25 percent of the income distribution. Heckman and Masterov (2004) compute income quartiles based on average family income when the children are between ages 6 and 10.

[13] Parental education is the highest level of education for the most educated parent as reported by the student.

[14] The NAEP tests have been administered since 1990, so the trends in the fraction at the basic level of proficiency can be tracked over time. These data show that there has been a decline since 1990 in the fraction scoring below basic on the eighth and twelfth grade mathematics tests and the eighth grade reading test, but the share below basic has increased over time for the twelfth grade reading test (Wirt et al., 2004).

pared by parents' education level at twelfth grade (Braswell et al., 2001; Grigg et al., 2003). The same pattern also holds when students are compared by a measure of the family's economic status at either eighth or twelfth grade (U.S. Department of Education, 2004a, 2004b; Braswell et al., 2001; Grigg et al., 2003).[15]

Other manifestations of problems in school achievement include special education placement, grade repetition, and dropping out of school. In each case, the incidence of these outcomes is higher for more-disadvantaged children. For example, rates of special education use fall steadily as income rises, from 18 percent for children in families with less than $15,000 in annual income to 6 percent for those in families making $75,000 or more.[16] Likewise, the incidence of ever having been retained in a grade for young people ages 16 to 24 is twice as high among families with incomes in the bottom 20 percent of the income distribution compared with those in the top 20 percent (18 percent versus 9 percent).[17] The chances of dropping out of high school are also higher for at-risk youth, such as those in single-parent families and those whose parents have less schooling themselves (Haveman and Wolfe, 1994).[18]

Ultimately, limited skills and low educational attainment increase the likelihood of undesirable outcomes in adulthood. Low educational attainment is associated with reduced rates of employment, and with lower earnings when employed (Carneiro and Heckman, 2003). Among high school dropouts ages 16 to 24, for example, 44 percent are neither in school nor working, compared with 25 percent

---

[15] The NAEP tabulations also compare student outcomes based on whether or not they are eligible for a free or reduced price school lunch, an indicator of poverty status.

[16] These figures are for a sample of children ages 6 to 13 receiving special education during the 1999–2000 school year as reported in Wagner, Marder, and Blackorby (2002), Exhibit 3-10.

[17] These figures are for 16- to 24-year-olds in 1995. See U.S. Department of Education (1997), Table 24.

[18] In terms of the overall incidence of dropping out, data from the Current Population Survey in 2002 indicate that 13 percent of 18- to 24-year-olds, or 3.4 million young people, had dropped out of school without a high school diploma or equivalent (e.g., a GED). See U.S. Census Bureau (undated), Table A-5.

of high school graduates and 9 percent of college graduates at the same ages.[19] While some of these youth are looking for work and some of the young women are at home caring for children, many are idle. Use of social welfare programs is also higher among those with low educational attainment, as are crime rates. Among young adults ages 24 to 26, rates of participation in welfare in 2001 were about 1.5 times as high for high school dropouts as for high school graduates (7.4 percent versus 4.9 percent) and over 6 times as high for dropouts as for those who obtained some college education or more (7.4 percent versus 1.2 percent).[20] Likewise, estimates by Lochner and Moretti (2004) indicate a strong negative relationship between crime and educational attainment, a relationship that holds after adjusting for factors that could generate a spurious correlation.

These adverse outcomes during childhood and adulthood have consequences that extend beyond the lost potential (near- and long-term) for the affected children. Government outlays are higher as a result of higher special education costs, greater participation in social welfare programs, and higher rates of crime and delinquency. Government revenues and economic growth rates are lower as a result of lost employment and earnings potential. These economic costs can be sizable, especially when they are considered in the context of the full life course. Estimates by Cohen (1988), for instance, indicate that a high school dropout costs society $243,000 to $388,000 in present-value dollars over his or her lifetime, while a typical career criminal generates $1.3 to $1.5 million in present-value societal costs.[21]

Data such as those cited above point to a number of identifiable demographic and socioeconomic factors that put children at risk of poor developmental outcomes in early childhood and eventually poor

---

[19] See Wirt et al. (2004), Table 13-1.

[20] Based on data from the 2002 Current Population Survey as reported in Brown, Moore, and Bzostek (2003), Table 16. The education differentials are similar for receipt of food stamps.

[21] Present-value amounts are the sum of future dollar values where future values are discounted to the present at a constant annual rate. Such discounting recognizes that a dollar of benefits in the future is worth less than a dollar of benefits today.

school performance. Among those identified in the literature are living in poverty or welfare dependency, living in a single-parent household, having a mother with less than a high school education, and having parents who speak a language other than English at home (often termed "a linguistically isolated household") (Snow, Burns, and Griffin, 1998; Zill and West, 2001; Vandivere et al., 2004). Even controlling for these factors, some studies indicate that being in a minority race or ethnic group is an independent risk factor, along with being younger at the time of school entry (West, Denton, and Germino-Hausken, 2000).

The share of children at risk is not trivial. For the same ECLS-K cohort referenced above, 31 percent have one of the first four risk factors listed in the preceding paragraph, while an additional 16 percent have two or more risk factors (Zill and West, 2001). Within large cities (population over 250,000), exposure to multiple risk factors rises to 26 percent. Multiple risk factors, using the same four factors, are most prevalent among Latino children and African-American children (33 percent and 27 percent, respectively), compared with Asian (17 percent) or white children (6 percent). Children with multiple risk factors, on average, are most likely to experience developmental difficulties in early childhood along with poor educational outcomes after they enter school, although there will always be resilient children who do well despite various disadvantages.

The Promise of Early Childhood Interventions

The logic of early intervention is to compensate for the various factors that place children at risk of poor outcomes, with additional supports for the parents, children, or family as a unit that can affect a child directly through structured experiences or indirectly by enhancing the caregiving environment (Shonkoff and Phillips, 2000). If learning begets learning, then interventions at younger ages have the potential to generate cumulative benefits by altering a child's developmental trajectory (Heckman, 2000; Heckman and Masterov, 2004). We can now identify many of the factors that place substantial numbers of children at risk of poor performance in school and beyond, and we know that the consequences for these children while they are young and when they reach adulthood are significant for them and the rest of society. It is thus reasonable to ask whether it is possible to intervene early in the lives of children to improve their developmental trajectory and how much early intervention can improve outcomes. A related issue is whether the resources devoted to early childhood interventions are repaid over time through savings in government spending, higher government revenues, or benefits to program participants or other members of society.

To identify whether the promise of early childhood interventions can be realized, we are interested in answering the following questions:

- What is the range of strategies for intervening early in the lives of disadvantaged children?
- For programs that have strong scientific evaluations, what outcomes for participating children and their families are affected? How large are the effects, and what characteristics are associated with successful programs?
- Are the dollar costs associated with early childhood programs outweighed by the dollar value of future benefits?

We address these questions in the remainder of the report.

In the next chapter, we turn our attention to the range of strategies early childhood interventions use for counteracting the stressors children and families face in the first few years of life. We highlight key dimensions along which early childhood intervention programs vary and identify a subset of programs that meet our criteria for rigorous evaluation of program effects. We identify 16 programs with scientifically sound evidence concerning program effects that also measure those effects as of kindergarten entry or beyond. These programs provide the strongest evidence base from which to judge the benefits of early childhood interventions for school readiness, and when follow-up periods are long enough, for later success in school and in adulthood. Another four programs meet our evaluation criteria; however, because they have shorter follow-up periods, we categorize them as providing a more limited but still promising evidence base.

We focus on the effects of early childhood interventions in the third chapter, relying on the research evaluations for the 20 programs with a strong or promising evidence base. We take a closer look at the types of outcomes that these programs affect and discuss the relative magnitudes of these effects. We also review the evidence on what features of early childhood intervention programs are associated with better outcomes and undertake our own meta-analysis to examine whether program effects vary by intervention features across the programs we review.

In the fourth chapter, we examine the economic case for investing in early childhood programs. For some people, it may be sufficient to show that early childhood interventions improve the lives of participating children and families along the lines reviewed in Chapter Three. Others may want to be assured that these programs—a form of investment in children—can pay back their program costs through the dollar value of future benefits, where those benefits may accrue to the participants themselves, the government, or society more generally. Thus, in Chapter Four we consider the range of spillover benefits that early childhood programs may generate for various stakeholders, and review the evidence from benefit-cost studies available for a subset of the programs we examined in Chapters Two and Three. We also highlight some of the other potential economic and noneconomic benefits from early childhood programs that are typically not captured in benefit-cost analyses.

In the final chapter, we provide a summary of the key findings from our analysis with an enumeration of ten conclusions that pertain to the factors placing children at risk in the early years of life, the approaches to early childhood interventions to counteract those risks, the demonstrated effects of programs with rigorous evaluations, key features associated with more effective programs, and the economic benefits associated with programs that work. Important caveats and limitations of our knowledge base are discussed as well. These findings provide a guide for decisionmakers considering investments in early childhood interventions, highlighting both the proven results from prior efforts and the promise of future investments.

CHAPTER TWO

Strategies for Intervention

There is no single, uniform approach for intervening early in the lives of disadvantaged children to compensate for the factors that may impede healthy child development in the years before school entry. Indeed, strategies for early childhood intervention are highly variable. In this chapter, we review different approaches for addressing risks faced in early childhood through services provided to affected children and their families. We begin by briefly reviewing the theoretical underpinnings for interventions with disadvantaged children in the years prior to school entry. We then highlight various dimensions along which early intervention programs vary, dimensions that are combined to generate a wide array of program models.

Given our interest in understanding the benefits from such programs, we next turn our attention to programs that have been rigorously evaluated. We first highlight approaches to program evaluation that provide the greatest confidence that true program effects have been measured, as opposed to the influence of other confounding factors. Within the subset of programs with strong evaluations, we are particularly interested in programs with solid evidence of program effects beyond the early childhood period (i.e., at kindergarten entry or beyond). We view these programs—ones with scientifically sound evaluations and longer follow-up—as providing the most solid evidence. Based on these two criteria and several others, we identify 16 programs with what we refer to as a strong evidence base. Another four programs provide a promising evidence base given shorter-term follow-up results. We provide a summary of the key features of the 20 programs. The results from the evaluations of these programs, and inferences about the features of successful programs, are the subject of Chapter Three.

Theoretical Foundations of Early Childhood Intervention

Traditionally, children and their development were relegated to the domain of the parent and family, without formal outside interference. As American society became increasingly urbanized and industrialized in the nineteenth century, and with the increase in immigrant families in cities, early childhood interventions began to be seen as opportunities to help children who faced risk factors for typical development because of family and home characteristics (Karoly et al., 1998; Meisels and Shonkoff, 2000). Today, early childhood intervention focuses primarily on children deemed vulnerable to poor outcomes later in life.

Child development researchers have theorized about what factors contribute to risk for later problems. To provide greater clarity about the risks children face, Huffman, Mehlinger, and Kerivan (2001, p. 5) distinguish between three kinds of risk that have import for child outcomes: fixed markers, variable markers, and causal risk factors.

> A risk factor may be a "fixed marker," that is, one that cannot be demonstrated to change. A risk factor may be a "variable marker," that is, one that can be demonstrated to change, but when changed, does not alter the probability of the outcome. Finally, a risk factor may be a "causal risk factor," that is one that can be changed and, when changed, does alter the risk of the outcome.

As delineated, fixed and variable markers are not appropriate foci for targeted interventions, the former because they are not subject to change and the latter because, when changed, they do not alter the risk of poor individual child outcomes. Huffman, Mehlinger, and Kerivan (2001) argue that, although children may be identified as likely to benefit from intervention by using fixed and variable markers (e.g., low birthweight, family composition, low socioeconomic status), the *focus* of interventions should be to address the causal risk factors amenable to change (e.g., cognitive deficits, parenting skills, behavior problems) that, when altered, lead to changes in the outcomes of interest.

Evidence suggests that early learning is cumulative and that basic early childhood skills are a necessary foundation for learning other skills in school (Whitehurst and Lonigan, 1998; Heckman, 2000; Landry, 2005). If so, providing intervention to at-risk children as early as possible will help prepare them for school entry and school demands, with the potential for subsequent benefits in terms of school performance, educational attainment, and adult economic outcomes. This inference is supported by research on brain development in young children and the idea of sensitive periods for developmental growth (Shore, 1997; Nelson, 2000; Shonkoff and Phillips, 2000; Huffman, Mehlinger, and Kerivan, 2001; Landry, 2005). Evidence also shows that early intervention has the potential to generate cost savings by preventing later problems that would otherwise require remediation (Karoly et al., 1998; Barnett, 2000).

Strategies for Early Childhood Intervention

Two types of early childhood intervention strategies—preschool and home visitation—are perhaps the most commonly known and most studied to date. Preschool is offered as an educational intervention specifically to help three- and four-year-old children gain emergent literacy and pre-math skills necessary for entry into kindergarten. At the same time, the preschool classroom serves as a place for children to form friendships, learn to get along with other children, and regulate their own behavior so as to develop appropriate socioemotional behaviors that will facilitate later learning (Huffman, Mehlinger, and Kerivan, 2001). Whereas preschool focuses almost exclusively on the child, home visitation is viewed as a two-generational approach in which professionals work with parents to help them support their infants, toddlers, and young children (Sweet and Appelbaum, 2004). The home visitation model first implemented in Elmira, New York, now operating across the country as the Nurse-Family Partnership (NFP) program, specifically focuses on the mother as the target for preventive intervention—in her role as a parent and as an individual (Olds, Eckenrode, et al., 1997; Olds, Kitzman, et al., 1997).[1]

These classic models of intervention are well known, but even within a given model, programs vary in many ways. For instance, preschool can be public or private, center- or school-based, can enroll children at risk for school readiness or have universal enrollment. Home visitation programs include the well-documented "Olds" model that uses professionally trained nurses and a uniform service delivery method,[2] but they also include programs that use paraprofessionals or other lay staff to deliver a mix of services tailored to the specific community. Gomby, Culross, and Behrman (1999) note that thousands of diverse home visitation programs are in operation. Furthermore, home visitation is often merely one component of a multi-faceted intervention program, such as Early Head Start.[3]

However, preschool and home visitation are not the only types of early intervention.[4] Our review of such interventions reveals that early intervention programs vary on different dimensions, so it is difficult to claim that there are specific strategies. Rather, early intervention programs are typically an amalgam of approaches. The key

---

[1] The NFP program was originally known as the Prenatal/Early Infancy Project (PEIP) when it was first implemented and evaluated in Elmira, New York.

[2] For additional details on the NFP developed by David Olds and colleagues, see Table A.1 in the appendix.

[3] Information and citations for the Abecedarian program and Early Head Start can be found in Table A.1.

[4] For other reviews of early childhood interventions, see Barnett (1995), Yoshikawa (1995), Karoly et al. (1998), Perloff et al. (1998), Gomby, Culross, and Behrman (1999), Shonkoff and Phillips (2000), Brooks-Gunn, Berlin, and Fuligni (2000), Currie (2001), Brown and Scott-Little (2003), Nelson, Westhues, and MacLeod (2003), Blau and Currie (2004), Ramey and Ramey (2004), Strickland and Barnett (2004), and Sweet and Appelbaum (2004).

dimensions of variation in early intervention programs, as summarized in Table 2.1, include the following:

- **Outcomes targeted for improvement.** The design of any intervention is driven by the outcomes for which improvements are desired within the targeted group. Child outcomes that programs aim to improve vary from school readiness skills to long-term school or economic success. For parents, they may also include economic success as well as pregnancy outcomes and childrearing skills. Depending on the outcomes of interest, the other dimensions of early childhood interventions follow, typically driven by a theory of change (Shonkoff and Phillips, 2000).[5]
- **Target person(s).** While early childhood programs by definition address the needs of children, not all programs consider the child as the primary target for services. Some programs target the family, specifically the parent, for intervention to improve outcomes for the child of interest. Often the target is the parent-child dyad: The parent is provided with parenting education and resources to better understand appropriate child development and how she or he can foster it.
- **Targeting criteria.** Different types of children and families may be identified for intervention services based on composition (e.g., single parent), ethnicity, mother's age, or other characteristics. A common criterion in intervention targeting is low-income or low socioeconomic status (SES) families. Children may be targeted based on an assessment of high risk for developmental difficulties (due to family circumstances or visible problems such as behavioral issues, low IQ, or low birthweight). Families may be targeted based on parental problems, such as low education or substance abuse.

---

[5] A theory of change is a theoretical model that links the strategies of intervention with the program goals. The theoretical models draw on models of human development such as the transactional model of Sameroff and Chandler (1975) and the ecological model of Bronfenbrenner (1979), among others (Shonkoff and Phillips, 2000).

Table 2.1
Key Dimensions of Early Childhood Intervention Programs

Dimension	Examples
Outcomes targeted for improvement	Pregnancy outcomes (parent)
	Cognitive)
	Socioemotional) "School
	Behavioral) readiness"
	Health)
	Economic (parent or child)
	Parent education (e.g., literacy)
	Parenting skills
Target person(s)	Child
	Parent
	Child-parent dyad
	Family unit
Targeting criteria	Child or family characteristics (minority or immigrant status, single-parent family, mother's age, first-time parents)
	Low-SES or low-income families
	Child health problems (e.g., low birthweight)
	Child cognitive problems (e.g., low IQ)
	Child behavioral problems
	Child assessed as high-risk (e.g., for developmental delay)
	Parental problems (e.g., substance use, low education, psychological, divorce, child abuse or neglect)
	Relationship or social problems (parent-child, child-peers, child-adults, parent-parent)
	Universal
Age of focal child	Prenatal to age 5, for shorter or longer age spans
Location of services	Home
	Non-home (center, school, medical setting)
Services offered	Educational (e.g., preschool, parenting education)
	Family supports (e.g., links to social services)
	Health- or nutrition-related
	Job-related
	Therapeutic
Intensity of intervention	Starting age to ending age
	Hours per week
	Weeks per year
Individualized attention	Individuals
	Small or large group
Program reach	National
	Statewide
	Citywide
	Single setting

- **Age of focal child.** Early childhood programs differ widely on the targeted age for the focal child in an intervention program. Intervention can start before birth (targeting the expectant mother) or as late as the fifth or sixth year of childhood. Some programs provide services over a span of years within the 0–5 age range; others focus service delivery on a narrow time window.

- **Location of services.** Programs differ in their approaches to reaching children and families who will benefit from services. Home visitation programs by nature serve children and families in their home setting. Other programs operate in a non-home setting such as a child care center, school, or medical facility. Mixed modes are used as well. Some primarily non-home programs also include a home component at some point in their service provision.

- **Services offered.** As mentioned, programs differ in what they offer families in the way of specific services, and program design is based on the outcomes each program is intended to improve. Some are designed solely to provide educational services to prepare children for school entry, so they will most likely offer child development or preschool programs for children. Such programs may also include other services such as health screening or nutrition services to supplement the educational curriculum. Other programs are interested in the overall functioning of the family, so they will offer a more holistic range of family support services to children and their families. Services for the target group may be very narrow or quite broad in any program. Moreover, a standard package of services may be offered to all children and parents who receive program intervention, or the set of services may be tailored for each child or family based on individual assessment.

- **Intensity of intervention.** The frequency and duration of services can vary substantially between early childhood programs. While a preschool program such as Head Start may be operational five days a week for four to eight hours a day over most of the year, a home visitation program may offer a one- or two-hour visit once a month or so. Considering differences in the starting and ending ages of participation in the program, the total hours of services delivered can vary significantly. Depending on the type of outcome desired, differences in intensity of interventions can have an important effect on outcomes.

- **Individualized attention.** Related to the frequency and intensity of services is the issue of whether children and families receive individualized attention or participate in groups. Individualized attention, such as home visits, requires more program resources and is likely to occur with less frequency but with more specifically targeted services. Programs serving groups, such as child care programs or parenting classes, can offer more hours of service with the trade-off of perhaps less individualized attention. In group settings, the number of participants per provider (e.g., child-teacher ratios in center-based settings) also affect the attention each participant receives. Again, the desired program outcomes dictate which trade-offs are made to achieve the program's goals.

- **Program reach.** Many interventions have been initiated in a single location based on local circumstances and funding availability. Several well-studied interventions were implemented in a single location to control the fidelity of the services to the program model and to conduct a rigorous evaluation. Other programs either have begun as national demonstration projects and then continued on a large scale or have started in a localized area and then been replicated in more locations. In some cases, larger-scale replication has been implemented with high fidelity to the original intervention model; others have been replicated with less fidelity and more local autonomy in determining community service needs, so they are only loosely based on the original model.

Research and practice in early childhood demonstrate that there is great heterogeneity of programs in existence. Most programs use some blend of the dimensions shown in Table 2.1 in defining their approach, and this often results in wide disparity between any two locally implemented interventions. Consequently, it is often difficult to claim that because Program A delivers some services similar to Program B, Program A will have the same outcomes as Program B. Much depends on the exact combination of services, who delivers the services, and the characteristics of the population served. This is often a result of unique features of the community in which programs are administered. A program focused entirely on home visitation for at-risk two-year-olds may be very different from a home visitation component of a multifaceted family literacy program. Importantly, not every early intervention program might be effective. The mix of program dimensions, population served, and outcomes of interest plays a critical role.

Strategies for Program Evaluation

To understand which programs are effective, a rigorous evaluation is necessary that isolates the effects of the program on child and family outcomes from other influential factors.[6] For example, a preschool program may produce graduates who are well prepared to enter school. However, without an evaluation that compares this group of children with similar children who did not receive the same preschool services, we cannot tell whether the children who attended preschool would have done well even without the program. We do not want to attribute a positive effect to a program without a comparison with what would have happened in the absence of the program, holding all other factors constant. Ultimately, we want to be able to answer the question "Compared to what?" to determine whether a program is effective. We are interested in the baseline against which we are comparing results.

The most rigorous form of evaluation is the randomized experiment, which is often referred to as the *gold standard*. In the con-

---

[6] For a more detailed discussion of evaluation approaches for causal inference, refer to Shadish, Cook, and Campbell (2001), and in relation to preschool programs, Karoly and Bigelow (2005).

text of early childhood interventions, this type of evaluation takes a group of children (or parents/families) who are eligible for a specific program and randomly assigns individuals to either the intervention (i.e., treatment) group, whose members participate in the program, or the comparison (i.e., control) group, whose members receive the normal program or no program at all for the given situation. This allows the analyst to isolate the effects of the program by comparing outcomes for individuals who are similar in all respects except for the intervention. In other words, since we cannot compare outcomes with and without a program for the same individual, the experimental design allows us to compare average outcomes for a group of individuals who are the same, on average, except that one group participated in the program and the other did not.[7]

Experimental evaluations are often difficult to conduct because of resource constraints or ethical concerns about withholding treatment from eligible groups. Therefore, quasi-experimental evaluations can be used to create comparison groups for evaluation purposes. While less rigorous than experiments, quasi-experiments can often be designed with comparison groups that allow for sound findings, sometimes with the addition of statistical techniques. A common quasi-experimental comparison group consists of children or families who are similar to the intervention group but live in an area where the program is not available or who are on a waiting list for an over-subscribed program.[8] Thus, these people are not being purposefully denied the intervention because of random assignment. They form a good counterfactual to the intervention because they are likely candidates for the intervention but do not receive services, and their inclu-

---

[7] The validity of an experimental evaluation can be compromised by a number of factors, including errors in the randomization process and nonrandom attrition from the study population. Experiments with small sample sizes have low statistical power to detect small effects compared with experiments with larger samples.

[8] Other quasi-experimental designs have also been used to evaluate early intervention programs. Among the programs we review below, other approaches include using siblings as a comparison group (i.e., one sibling attends preschool and the other does not) or using the "accident" of birth date as a type of natural experiment that determines which children enter a program and which do not. See Karoly and Bigelow (2005) for further discussion.

sion or exclusion does not depend on the parents' actions. (Where participation versus nonparticipation depends on the parents' choice, the outcome of the intervention may be confounded with the result of good parenting.) The objective is that the two groups are generally similar before the intervention starts (that is, on such observable factors as family income, ethnicity, parental education level, etc., as well as other unobservable factors, such as parent motivation) or that any differences are controlled for in a statistical analysis to the extent possible. If this objective is achieved, a comparison of outcomes for the two groups after the program should indicate the effects of the program compared with no program intervention.

Evaluations that do not use a comparison group suffer from weaknesses that do not allow confidence that estimated program effects actually capture the effectiveness of the program compared with no program. For example, an early intervention evaluation that measures outcomes for children before and after a program will tell us how far the children have advanced over that time period, but it does not allow us to claim with certainty that those gains would not have been made in the absence of the program. Likewise, comparing children in a given program with national or other averages does not confirm that those children would not have compared as well (or as poorly) without program intervention.

Early Childhood Intervention Programs with Rigorous Evaluations and Strong Evidence to Date

To determine which programs show evidence of effectiveness in preparing children for school and improving subsequent outcomes, we scanned the early childhood literature to identify relevant early intervention programs that have been implemented and evaluated.[9] We considered programs included in prior meta-analyses, narrative syn-

---

[9] Of course, programs with any form of evaluation represent just a subset of the many programs that have been implemented in various communities around the United States.

theses, and other reviews.[10] In addition, we queried the *PNC Grow Up Great* Advisory Council. We focused our efforts on intervention programs that have been implemented and evaluated in the United States since 1960.[11] We identified just under 40 such early childhood intervention programs, which we subjected to several criteria to identify programs for further analysis.

The criteria we used to select programs for further analysis fall into three categories: (1) they implement early childhood interventions as we have defined them for this study; (2) they focus on outcomes of interest for our study; and (3) they have rigorous evaluations. Criteria falling under (1) were the following:

- The program must intervene sometime during the period from nine months before birth to age 5.
- The program must include a child development focus in some way.
- The program must not focus primarily on special-needs children.

The first criterion limits our focus to programs that serve children in the years before kindergarten entry. The second excludes some early childhood interventions whose primary objective is improving outcomes other than child cognitive or socioemotional development. For example, we did not include programs that aim purely to promote a child's physical health. Programs serving children with special needs may differ in important ways, so we also exclude them from our analysis.

Two selection criteria relate to the outcomes studied in the program evaluation:

---

[10] These studies included Barnett (1995), Yoshikawa (1995), Karoly et al. (1998), Perloff et al. (1998), Gomby, Culross, and Behrman (1999), Currie (2001), Brown and Scott-Little (2003), Nelson, Westhues, and MacLeod (2003), Aos et al. (2004), Blau and Currie (2004), Strickland and Barnett (2004), and Sweet and Appelbaum (2004).

[11] Studies implemented outside the United States or before 1960 are less likely to be relevant for understanding the effects of programs implemented in the United States today and in the future.

- The program must focus on at least one child outcome for measurement, regardless of the target person for services.
- The program evaluation must include follow-up information at approximately kindergarten entry, age 5 or later (i.e., not just an evaluation of results at age 2, 3, or 4).

The first criterion ensures that the study measured one or more child outcomes. While we are primarily interested in child outcomes, we also recognize that there are inputs and intermediary outcomes (or precursors) for these final child outcomes, consistent with the model shown in Figure 2.1. For our analysis, we include only programs that measure directly what we refer to in the figure as "final child outcomes" (e.g., age-appropriate literacy skills), not merely inputs (e.g., parent reads to child) or intermediary outcomes (e.g., emergent literacy such as recognizing letters or knowing that text reads from left to right). The second criterion ensures that children are followed long enough to show meaningful effects for school readiness and beyond. Programs that do not have follow-up data at kindergarten entry or beyond are included in our group of "promising" programs because they show early results, but we do not know for certain that these effects translate into school readiness skills as measured at school entry or later.

Finally, three selection criteria are relevant for ensuring a strong evaluation design:

- The program evaluation must use a properly implemented experimental or quasi-experimental design that includes, at a minimum, a well-matched comparison group with appropriate statistical controls.
- The sample size in both the treatment and comparison groups must be at least 20 persons.
- The evaluation must be formally published and publicly available.

Figure 2.1
Examples of Influences on Child Outcomes

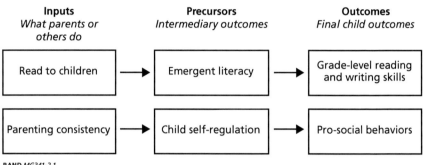

RAND *MG341-2.1*

Among these methodology-related criteria, the first gives us reasonable confidence that the estimated program effects are true causal effects. The second eliminates studies that have low statistical power to detect significant program effects. In other words, we do not want to err by concluding that a program is ineffective when it simply did not have a sufficient sample to detect moderate-sized impacts with reasonable chance. The final criterion ensures that the research results are readily available for assessing the quality of the research methodology. For most of the programs we review, the results are published in peer-reviewed journals.

Applying these criteria to the original set of evaluations, we identified 20 programs for consideration in this analysis (see Table 2.2). (One intervention, Project CARE [Carolina Approach to Responsive Education], contributes two program models, given the design of the evaluation as discussed below.) Sixteen programs met all our criteria, and four additional programs met all criteria except longitudinal information at age 5 or later. These latter four programs evaluated children as late as ages 2 or 3, and all had at least one statis-

Table 2.2
Early Childhood Intervention Programs Included in Study

Programs with a Strong Evidence Base

Carolina Abecedarian Project

Chicago Child-Parent Centers (CPC)

Comprehensive Child Development Program (CCDP)

DARE to be You

Early Training Project (ETP)

Head Start

High/Scope Perry Preschool Project

HIPPY (Home Instruction Program for Preschool Youngsters) USA

Houston Parent-Child Development Center (PCDC)

Incredible Years

Infant Health and Development Program (IHDP)

Nurse-Family Partnership (NFP)

Oklahoma Pre-K

Project CARE (Carolina Approach to Responsive Education) (2 models)

Syracuse Family Development Research Program (FDRP)

Programs with a Promising Evidence Base[a]

Developmentally Supportive Care: Newborn Individualized
Developmental Care and Assessment Program (DSC/NIDCAP)

Early Head Start

Parents as Teachers

Reach Out and Read

---

[a] Programs are classified as "promising" because a substantial number of children were as young as age 2 or 3 at the time of the last follow-up.

tically significant result.[12] In most cases, programs that we originally considered were excluded from our final analysis because they did not meet our criteria for a child development focus, at least one child development measure, and/or a rigorous evaluation design.

We note that, unlike other synthesis studies, we did not require a minimum effect size or statistically significant results in identifying the 16 programs that met all our criteria. Both effective and ineffective programs are included among those that meet the full set of criteria above. *Effective programs* are those that had at least one outcome finding at the 5-percent significance level. *Ineffective programs* are those with a sound evaluation but no statistically significant results related to child development (i.e., our two criteria for study outcomes). The inclusion of ineffective programs allows us to examine the possible role of various program characteristics in generating larger program effects. In other words, including both ineffective and effective programs allows us to examine the relationship between program features and program effects with a wider range than we would observe if we limited our set of programs to only those that are effective.

Table 2.3 summarizes key features of the associated evaluations for the 20 programs we examine: the first year of the program evaluation, whether the study used a random assignment or quasi-experimental design, the initial sample sizes for experimental/treatment and control/comparison groups, and the ages at follow-up. (See Appendix A for a brief summary of each program and the citations for the program's evaluation.)

As indicated in Table 2.3, the earliest program evaluations began in the early 1960s, while the latest took place in the early 2000s. Seventeen of the 20 programs use an experimental design for the pro-

---

[12] The Healthy Steps program is an example of a program we did not include in our study. While this program was rigorously evaluated, it focused on child physical health rather than cognitive or socioemotional outcomes (see Minkovitz et al., 2003, and Zuckerman et al., 2004). The difference between the treatment and comparison group for the one cognitive outcome (child language development assessed as of age 2) was not statistically significant.

Table 2.3
Features of the Evaluations for Selected Early Childhood Intervention Programs

Program (Initial Evaluation Year)	Study Design	Initial Sample	Ages at Follow-Up
Programs with a Strong Evidence Base			
Abecedarian (1972)	RA	E = 57 C = 54	5, 8, 12, 15, 21
Chicago CPC (1983)	QE	E = 1,150 C = 389	6, 9, 10, 11, 14, 21
CCDP (1990)	RA	E = 2,213 C = 2,197	5
DARE to be You (1991)	RA	E = 285 C = 189	4–6
ETP (1962)	RA	E = 44 C = 21	5, 6, 7, 8, 10, 16–20
Head Start (1967)	RA and QE	E* = 87 to 1,553 C* = 86 to 6,234	3, 4, 5, 6, 10–16, 23, 18–30
Perry Preschool (1962)	RA	E = 58 C = 65	5–11, 14, 15, 19, 27, 40
HIPPY USA (1990)	RA	Cohort 1: E = 37, C = 32 Cohort 2: E = 47, C = 66	5–6
Houston PCDC (1970)	RA	E = 90 C = 201	3, 4–7, 8–11
Incredible Years (mid-1990s)	RA	E* = 47 to 345 C* = 48 to 167	4–6
IHDP (1985)	RA	E = 377 C = 608	3, 5, 8
NFP (1978)	RA	E* = 116 to 245 C* = 184 to 515	3, 4, 6, 15
Oklahoma Pre-K (2001)	QE	EV1: E = 1,112, C = 1,284 EV2: E = 1,461, C = 1,567	4 or 5
Project CARE (1978)	RA	E1 = 17, E2 = 25 C = 23	4 1/2
Syracuse FDRP (1969)	QE	E = 108 C = 108	5, 6, 15

Table 2.3—continued

Program (Initial Evaluation Year)	Study Design	Initial Sample	Ages at Follow-Up
Programs with a Promising Evidence Base			
DSC/NIDCAP (1979)	RA and QE	EV1: E = 124, C = 131 EV2: C = 21, E = 24	2
Early Head Start (1995)	RA	E = 1,513 and C = 1,488	1, 2, 3
Parents as Teachers (1991)	RA	E* = 60 to 298 C* = 60 to 329	2, 3
Reach Out and Read (1996)	RA	EV1: E = 65, C = 70 EV2: E = 106, C = 99	2–6

SOURCE: Authors' tabulations based on sources cited in Appendix A.

NOTES: See Table 2.2 for full program names. RA = random assignment; QE = quasi-experimental; E = experimental or treatment group; E1/E2 = experimental group 1 or 2 in a multi-arm design; C = control or comparison group; EV1 = evaluation 1; EV2 = evaluation 2.

*Indicates three or more studies with range of sample sizes as indicated.

gram evaluation (again counting Project CARE as two programs).[13] Although the studies using a quasi-experimental design are among the best nonexperimental evaluations of early childhood interventions, it is possible that the three studies in this category are subject to potential biases—most likely in the direction of generating more favorable results—that are less likely for the experimental designs.[14] To the ex-

---

[13] We note that a nationally representative experimental evaluation of the Head Start program, the Head Start Impact Study, is currently under way (see U.S. Department of Health and Human Services, 2005).

[14] The results from quasi-experimental studies would be biased upward (i.e., they would generate effects that are larger than the true program effects) to the extent that early intervention program participants are selected from among those who would be more likely to succeed even in the absence of the intervention. This would be the case, for example, if parents who are more highly motivated to see their children succeed are more likely to enroll their children in the intervention. The quasi-experimental studies reported in Table 2.3 use the most sophisticated statistical methods designed to control for such selection effects, but some upward bias may still remain.

tent this is an issue in the chapters that follow, we will consider the sensitivity of our inferences to the inclusion or exclusion of findings from these nonexperimental studies.

However, even random assignment studies may suffer from problems of implementation that subject them to various biases. Among the evaluations listed in Table 2.3, the Comprehensive Child Development Program (CCDP) has been criticized for shortcomings in the implementation of its experimental design and the associated evaluation (see the discussion in Gilliam et al., 2000). The CCDP study utilized random assignment and included very large sample sizes, but, as we discuss in the next chapter, the program evaluation did not find significant effects on the child outcomes of interest. Critics have suggested that results from this study should not inform early childhood policy because the study evaluated only participants in the start-up year of the program. There are also questions about the comparability of the treatment and control groups, and there are a variety of other possible explanations for the null findings. Despite these weaknesses in the evaluation, we include the study in our analysis because it still ranks among the strongest early childhood evaluations. As we discuss in the next chapter, we examine the sensitivity of our statistical analysis to the inclusion or exclusion of this study given these methodological concerns.

In several cases, the intervention programs listed in Table 2.3 have been evaluated for more than one cohort of participants in alternative settings in order to assess the ability to replicate findings. For example, the NFP program has been evaluated in a sequence of experimental studies in Elmira, New York; Memphis, Tennessee; and Denver, Colorado, with variation in the characteristics of population served in each site.[15] The Carolina Abecedarian Project, Project CARE (with the ECE component, discussed further below), and Infant Health and Development Program (IHDP) implemented a closely related program model in a total of ten sites, although they each used a different targeting approach and the ages at which the

---

[15]For NFP, Table 2.3 shows the range of sample sizes that applies across the three trials.

intervention ended varied. Favorable effects found in alternative settings and with different population groups, as discussed further in the next chapter, provide greater confidence that the measured effects are generalizable.

The table also indicates that ages at follow-up cover a wide range. As noted above, many or all of the children were as young as age 2 or 3 in four of the studies. Of the remaining 16 studies (where Project CARE contributes two studies), seven follow children through age 6 at most; another two follow participants a year or two longer, up to the end of elementary school (age 11). Two more programs followed children to age 15. Four programs have follow-up periods that extend into young adulthood (early to late 20s); one program (Perry Preschool) recently completed a follow-up of participants when they were age 40.

With two exceptions, the program evaluations listed in Table 2.3 assessed the effect of a single program design—a fixed bundle of services. In the first case, Project CARE, the experimental design included two treatment groups, one that received home visits and full-day year-round center-based early childhood education (ECE) and a second that received home visits only.[16] This evaluation design allows for a direct comparison of the difference in effects between two program models (with and without the ECE component in this case), as well as the effect of either model relative to a control group. In the second case, the Denver trial of the NFP program, one experimental group was served by nurse home visitors; the second experimental group was served by paraprofessional home visitors. As we discuss further in the next chapter, the paucity of studies with this type of de-

---

[16] The Carolina Abecedarian Project also included a multi-arm treatment design, but it applied after children reached age 5 when they entered kindergarten. At that time, children in the treatment and control groups were randomly assigned to either a school-age intervention through age 8 or a control group. This design allows for a comparison of the impacts of an early childhood intervention program combined with a school-age intervention versus the early childhood intervention alone or the school-age intervention alone. Each program variant can also be compared with the control group that received no services over the entire age span. The Chicago CPC program also provides for continued services past kindergarten entry, which has been evaluated relative to a preschool-only program. For information on both evaluations, see the citations in Appendix A.

sign means that we have little experimental evidence on the differential effect of a given program feature or service. Instead, we know more about the effect of specific bundles of features and services as they are combined in a given program model.

There are also differences across programs in the experiences of children in the control or comparison group—the baseline program the intervention is compared with. Notably, Abecedarian, Project CARE, and the IHDP provided a baseline set of health, family, or developmental services to the control group. For example, all children in both the control and treatment groups of the IHDP received medical, developmental, and social assessments, with referral to further care as appropriate (IHDP, 1990). To the extent that the basic services received by the control group also confer benefits on the children or their families, the measured program effects will be attenuated from what they would have been if the program had been compared with a baseline that did not include such services. Given the differences in baselines in the various programs we review, care must be taken when interpreting any differences in the magnitudes of effects across programs.

An important caveat to this list of programs is that they are not intended to represent the full range of early intervention programs or even of effective early intervention programs. Rather, they are those that have been rigorously evaluated to date and that report, in published outlets, measures at age 5 or later. Several well-known programs did not meet all our criteria; lack of a rigorous evaluation was a primary reason. It is noteworthy that many early childhood intervention programs have been implemented but not rigorously evaluated, so we are unable to assess their effectiveness compared with an appropriate counterfactual. This study examines only those programs whose results concerning school readiness and later success in school and beyond we are confident in appraising. We recognize that it does not include the full universe of early childhood interventions.

Moreover, we acknowledge that there may exist a greater propensity to publish studies with positive and significant findings compared with studies with no significant differences or negative findings. One might also expect the likelihood of continued follow-up of the long-term effects of an early childhood intervention to be higher for those programs that initially produce favorable results. This potential for "publication bias" or even "follow-up bias" would mean that we are not reporting on a representative sample of early childhood intervention programs or even early childhood intervention programs with rigorous evaluations. If, indeed, mostly favorable findings are published, it should not be taken to mean that all early childhood programs will achieve results similar to those we consider in this study. Rather, the results can be viewed as illustrative of the outcomes that may be affected and the magnitude of those effects.[17]

A further issue is that nine of the 20 programs are not currently in operation in the same configuration as they were when evaluated. Several of the most rigorously evaluated interventions listed above were implemented as one-time interventions with small groups of children 20 or more years ago. At that time, the counterfactual to an early childhood intervention such as high-quality preschool was no intervention at all. Today, however, many at-risk children are targeted for some form of early childhood intervention before age 5. Thus, the counterfactual to any single intervention today is likely to be some other form of intervention. This complicates the comparison of effects across programs (such as their magnitude) because the experiences of the comparison groups may have changed over time. Moreover, the inability to replicate the exact conditions of programs implemented and evaluated several decades ago makes it harder to ensure that program impacts would be the same today even if the program were implemented the same way. In some cases, program effects might be stronger; in other cases, they might be weaker.

---

[17] Some might argue that, given enough evaluations, a few will produce significant effects by chance even if early childhood interventions are equivalent to a placebo. However, each of the programs we review is based on an underlying theory of change grounded in the theoretical child development literature. The consistency across studies and the robustness of results over time for a given study population suggest that the results we report on are unlikely due to chance factors.

Taxonomy of Selected Early Childhood Intervention Programs

Table 2.4 lists all 20 programs and describes their key features at the time they were evaluated, according to the dimensions shown in Table 2.1. A review of the features of the 20 programs in Table 2.4 shows that, despite variation in the dimensions of each individual program, they fall into a few distinct patterns. Based on these patterns, we have classified our 20 programs into one of three program approaches as illustrated in Figure 2.2.[18] (The time dimension illustrated in the figure is addressed below.) The three approaches are

- home visiting or parent education
- home visiting or parent education combined with early childhood education ("combination programs")
- early childhood education only.

The first group consists of eight programs that focus on delivering a set of services to parents and, in some cases, to children as well, through either home visits or parent education delivered in another setting, such as a classroom. The first five programs employ home visits: NFP; Developmentally Supportive Care: Newborn Individualized Developmental Care and Assessment Program (DSC/NIDCAP); Parents As Teachers; Project CARE (with no ECE) and HIPPY (Home Instruction Program for Preschool Youngsters) USA. The remaining three programs—Reach Out and Read, DARE to be You, and Incredible Years—focus on parent education.

The second group, the largest, contains 11 programs that combine home visits or other ways of providing parent education (in either a center or home setting) with early childhood education services delivered to the children. We refer to these programs as "combination programs." In most of them, the bulk of resources is directed toward providing the ECE services for children. Home visits and parent edu-

---

[18] For other classification schemes of early childhood intervention programs, see St. Pierre, Layzer, and Barnes (1995) and Perloff et al. (1998).

Table 2.4
Key Dimensions of Selected Early Childhood Intervention Programs

Program	Goals	Target Person(s)	Targeting Criteria	Age of Focal Child	Location of Services
Programs with a Strong Evidence Base					
Abecedarian	Determine whether early childhood education can prevent retarded development of high-risk children	Child and parent	High score on high-risk index (developmental delays and school failure)	Entry: 6 weeks to 3 months Exit: 5 to 8 years	Home and child care center
Chicago CPC	Promote cognitive and socioemotional development to prepare child for school entry and beyond	Child and parent	Low-income, high-poverty neighborhood, not served by Head Start	Entry: 3 to 4 years Exit: 6 to 9 years	Pre-school and school (public schools)
CCDP	Enhance child development and help families achieve economic self-sufficiency	Child and parent	Low-income	Entry: Prenatal to 1 year Exit: 6 years	Various (e.g., center, home, office)
DARE to be You	Improve parenting skills and child development in ways that contribute to children's resiliency to substance use later in life	Child and parent	High-risk families with children between ages 2 and 5	Entry and exit: 2 to 5 years	Center
ETP	Improve educability of young children from low-income families	Child	Low SES	Entry: 4 to 5 years Exit: 6 years	Preschool center and home

Services Offered	Intensity of Intervention	Individual or Group Attention	Program Reach	Program Currently Operating?
Home visits and educational child care	Full-day, daily, year-round child care; approximately biweekly home visits; school-age continuation services	Individual and group	One site in North Carolina	No
Preschool and elementary (K–3) programs, parent resources	Part-day preschool, school year; regular K–3 school day, school year; parent involvement in class half day per week	Individual and group	Chicago, Illinois	Yes
Multiple services, such as early childhood education and care, intensive case management, counseling, life skills training, referrals	Varied across families; on average, families participated for more than three years	Individual and group	Nationwide demonstration projects	No
Parent-child workshops with focus on parenting skills and developmentally appropriate children's activities	15 to 18 hours of parent training workshops and simultaneous children's programs, preferably in 10–12 week period	Group	Western states	Yes
Preschool and home visits	Part-day preschool in summer; weekly, year-round home visits	Individual and group	Murfreesboro, Tennessee	No

Table 2.4—continued

Program	Goals	Target Person(s)	Targeting Criteria	Age of Focal Child	Location of Services
Head Start	Increasing school readiness (cognitive, socio-emotional, and health) of children from low-income families	Child and parent	Low-income	Entry: 3 to 4 years Exit: 5 years	Pre-school center
Perry Preschool	Improve intellectual and social development of young children	Child	Low-income and low IQ scores	Entry: 3 to 4 years Exit: 5 years	Pre-school center and home
HIPPY USA	Help parents with limited education prepare their children for school entry	Parent	Low-income and low education	Entry: 3 to 4 years Exit: 5 years	Home and center
Houston PCDC	Help economically disadvantaged children perform better in school	Child and parent	Low-income and Mexican-American	Entry: 1 year (HV), 2 years (center) Exit: 3 years	Child care center and home
Incredible Years	Promote child social and emotional competence and address children's behavioral and emotional problems	Child and parent	Children at risk of or experiencing behavior problems	Entry and exit: 2 to 8 years	Center and school

Services Offered	Intensity of Intervention	Individual or Group Attention	Program Reach	Program Currently Operating?
Preschool and parent support and parenting programs	Part-day or full-day preschool, school-year or year-round, 1 or 2 years—varies across sites. Parent involvement varies considerably across sites	Individual and group	National	Yes
Preschool and home visits	Part-day, daily preschool and weekly home visits, school year, 1 or 2 years	Individual and group	Ypsilanti, Michigan	No
Parenting classes and books given to parents with activities to do with children; home visits	Parents meet with paraprofessionals biweekly for 45–60 minutes; parents meet with children using HIPPY materials at least 15 minutes daily; parents have group meetings biweekly; 30 weeks per year for two years	Individual and group	Multiple states	Yes
Home visits, parenting education, and Piagetian child care	Weekly home visits and four (2-day) family workshops for the first year; part-day (2 or 4 mornings a week) child care and monthly or biweekly evening discussions for parents for second year	Individual and group	Houston, Texas	No
Parenting classes and children's programs	Parents: 12–14 weeks, 2 hours per week; children: 18–20 weeks, 2 hours per week; teachers: 6 days (42 hours)	Group	Multiple states	Yes

Table 2.4—continued

Program	Goals	Target Person(s)	Targeting Criteria	Age of Focal Child	Location of Services
IHDP	Reduce developmental, behavioral, and other health problems	Child and parent	Low-birthweight, premature infants	Entry: birth (HV), 1 year (center) Exit: 36 months (adjusted for prematurity)	Home and child care center
NFP	Improve prenatal health and birth outcomes; improve child health, development, and safety; improve maternal life course outcomes	Parent	Low-income, unmarried, first-time mothers	Entry: up to 30th week of gestation Exit: 2 years	Home
Oklahoma Pre-K	Improve child development and school readiness	Child	Universal	Entry: 4 years Exit: 5 years	Pre-kindergarten center
Project CARE (no ECE)	Improve cognitive development for high-risk children	Child and parent	High score on high-risk index (developmental delays)	Entry: 4 to 6 weeks (HV) Exit: 5 years	Home
Project CARE (with ECE)	Improve cognitive development for high-risk children	Child and parent	High score on high-risk index (developmental delays)	Entry: 4 to 6 weeks (HV); 6 weeks to 3 months (center) Exit: 5 years	Home and child care center
Syracuse FDRP	Improve child and family functioning that sustains growth after intervention ceases	Child and parent	Low-income, low-education, young mothers	Entry: Last trimester (HV); 6 months (child care) Exit: 5 years	Home and family child care setting

Services Offered	Intensity of Intervention	Individual or Group Attention	Program Reach	Program Currently Operating?
Early childhood development programs and family support services	Home visits: weekly in year 1 and biweekly in years 2 and 3; child care center: daily, part or full-day starting at age 1; parent meetings: bimonthly beginning at 12 months	Individual and group	8 sites	No
Home visits by trained nurses (or paraprofessionals in one experimental site)	Home visit schedule follows developmental stages of pregnancy and early childhood (approximately 6–9 visits during pregnancy and 20 from birth to second birthday); postnatal visits average 1 hour and 15 minutes	Individual	Multiple states	Yes
Preschool program	Part-day and full-day programs, school year	Group	Oklahoma	Yes
Home visits (family education classes)	Family education: 2.5 visits per month (every 10 days)	Individual	One site in North Carolina	No
Child care and home visits (family education classes)	Child development center: Full-day, daily, year-round; family education: 2.5 visits per month (every 10 days)	Individual and group	One site in North Carolina	No
Home visits, parent training, and family child care	Weekly home visits; part-day child care (6–14 months); full-day child care (15–60 months) year-round	Individual and group	Syracuse, New York	No

Table 2.4—continued

Program	Goals	Target Person(s)	Targeting Criteria	Age of Focal Child	Location of Services
Programs with a Promising Evidence Base					
DSC/NIDCAP	Avoid develop-mental delays and mental/physical impair-ment	Child and parent	Preterm, low-birth-weight infants	Entry: birth Exit: 2 years	Hospital and home
Early Head Start	Promote healthy prenatal out-comes, enhance development of children ages 0 to 3, and support healthy family functioning	Child and parent	Low SES	Entry: pre-natal or child less than 1 year Exit: 3 years	Child care center and home
Parents as Teachers	Empower parents to give their chil-dren a good start in life, prepare children for school entry, and prevent and re-duce child abuse	Child and parent	Universal	Entry: prenatal or child less than 8 months Exit: 3 to 6 years	Home and center
Reach Out and Read	Encourage parents to read aloud to children to foster child literacy	Parent	Low SES	Entry: 6 months to 5 years Exit: 5 years	Pediatric doctor's office

SOURCE: Authors' tabulations based on sources cited in Appendix A.

NOTES: See Table 2.2 for full program names. HV = home visits; SES = socioeconomic status; ECE = early childhood education.

Services Offered	Intensity of Intervention	Individual or Group Attention	Program Reach	Program Currently Operating?
Intensive monitoring while in NICU, including neurobehavioral observation, and home visits afterward	NICU: two 25-minute therapy sessions daily Home visits twice monthly for one hour	Individual	National	Yes
Home visits, child development services, parenting education, child care, health and mental health care, and family support	Weekly home visits and at least 20 hours per week of center-based child care, or a combination of the two	Individual and group	National	Yes
Home visits by parent educators; group meetings with parents; developmental health, vision, and hearing screening; and building networks to meet family needs	Weekly to monthly home visits/group meetings, 60 to 90 minutes	Individual and group	National	Yes
Doctors and nurses give new books to parents at each well-child visit and provide advice about reading aloud with their child	Regularly scheduled well-child visits	Individual	National	Yes

Figure 2.2
Taxonomy of Early Childhood Intervention Programs

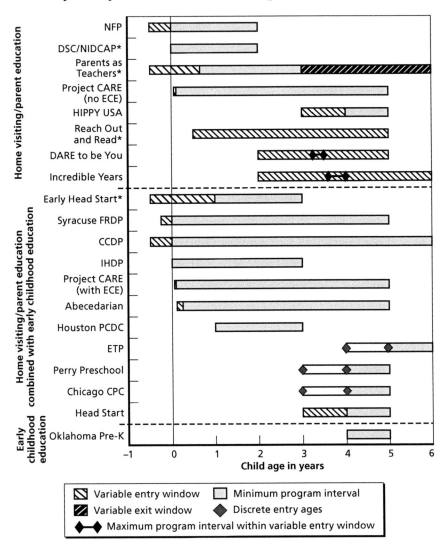

SOURCE: Authors' tabulations based on sources cited in Appendix A.
NOTES: See Table 2.2 for full program names. Programs with an asterisk are designated as having a promising evidence base because a substantial number of children were as young as age 2 or 3 at the time of the last follow-up. All other programs are designated as having a strong evidence base.
RAND MG341-2.2

cation are considered to be important components of the program, but these services are typically less resource intensive.

The third group includes one program that focuses on the child only through early childhood education: Oklahoma Pre-K, where services are delivered in preschool classrooms in public schools.

Figure 2.2 also highlights the timing of service delivery across the 20 programs and within the three program approaches. The reference point is the age of the focal child, shown on the bottom axis, which can begin as early as the prenatal period and continue through age 6.[19] Most programs do not have a fixed age range over which services are provided. Rather, the ages over which services are provided can vary across individual participants because the entry age, the exit age, or both can vary. Programs with a fixed program interval (both entry and exit age) are shown with a solid horizontal bar that marks the entry age and exit age, so the length of the bar indicates the number of years services are provided. When the entry window varies, that interval is shown with a diagonal striped pattern in the horizontal bar, while a variable exit window is shown with a diagonal striped, black-shaded pattern. In between the variable entry and exit windows is a light-shaded segment of the bar that represents the minimum program interval, i.e., the interval that extends from the last age of entry to the first age of exit. The maximum program interval thus extends from the earliest entry age to the last exit age, or the length of the bar segments combined. In three cases with formal preschool programs (ETP, Perry Preschool, and Chicago CPC), the entry age is discrete (i.e., age 3 or 4), designated by a dark-shaded diamond at the relevant ages. Two of the parent education programs (DARE to be You and Incredible Years) essentially have a three- or four-year entry window, but the services provided are limited to a fixed length (12 and 20 weeks, respectively). Those programs are marked with a horizontal line with black diamond endpoints located in the midpoint of the window over which entry can take place.

---

[19] Several of the programs in Figure 2.2 provided continuation services to children once they entered kindergarten or elementary school. This feature, which is relevant for the Abecedarian program, the Chicago CPC program, and Incredible Years, is not illustrated in the figure.

Among the eight programs that provide home visiting or parent education, the first four—all home visiting programs—begin as early as the prenatal period or within a few weeks of birth. For example, the NFP program is available to first-time mothers up to the 30th week of gestation, and services continue through age 2 of the focal child. Of the three parent education programs, Reach Out and Read potentially begins the earliest (at 6 months), with services delivered at discrete points during well-child visits at a pediatrician's office. The other two parent education programs begin as early as age 2, while the HIPPY USA home visiting program begins as early as age 3.

The programs using the middle approach, which combines home visiting or parent education with ECE, fall into two main groups. The first seven programs begin at some point up to age 1 (three programs as early as the prenatal period) and continue until at least age 3. Three programs provide services until the child reaches age 5 or 6. The final four programs in this group begin as preschool programs at ages 3, 4, or 5—one or two years before kindergarten entry. The one program that uses the ECE-only approach, Oklahoma Pre-K, is a one-year preschool program.

Beyond the program features highlighted in Figure 2.2, Table 2.4 reveals that the majority of programs target both the parent and child for intervention, and many of the programs utilize both home and non-home settings for service delivery. Only two of the programs use the home setting exclusively (NFP and Project CARE with no ECE); seven programs are located solely in non-home settings, which are more likely than not to be education settings. Most programs include an individualized component, although several provide services only in a group setting.

The bulk of the programs we identified target at-risk children or families rather than providing services universally; only Parents as Teachers and Oklahoma Pre-K are universal programs. However, this fact could be partially attributed to a bias in the types of programs evaluated because universal programs are more difficult to evaluate rigorously. Of the risk factors used to target the population served, low income or low SES is indicated for half of the programs. A significant percentage of children in the programs at the time programs were evaluated are from minority groups.

Almost all the programs have a fairly high intensity level and last a year or longer, with child care and preschool services offered daily and home visits generally conducted once a month or more. Only two of the programs (Incredible Years and DARE to be You) offer a short-term intervention of 42 hours or less over two to four months. At the other extreme, Project CARE and the Carolina Abecedarian Project provided year-round, full-time educational day care starting soon after birth and continuing through age 5. Although the CCDP covers an even longer age span, it delivers a less intensive set of services to children.

CHAPTER THREE

What Works in Early Childhood Intervention Programs

Early childhood intervention is now widely recognized as a promising approach to both improving the well being of participating children and families and reducing the demand for social services across the life course. Early childhood intervention is described as an "investment," and decisionmakers have proposed early childhood intervention as a prevention policy that pays for itself (Rolnick and Grunewald, 2003; CED, 2004). Although the logic of early childhood intervention is compelling, the question is whether there is evidence that intervention programs can improve the outcomes of participants and, if so, how much of a difference such programs make. Furthermore, as we saw in the previous chapter, early childhood intervention comes in a variety of shapes and sizes. To the extent that early intervention programs work, are there certain features that are associated with more-effective programs? We turn to these questions in this chapter, drawing on the evidence gained from the high-quality evaluations of the 20 programs we identified in Chapter Two.

We begin in the next section by reviewing the range of outcomes that early childhood interventions have been demonstrated to influence. These include outcomes both during the school-age years and in adulthood. Next we consider the magnitude of the effects across a range of outcomes, at younger and older ages. Finally, we assess the information available regarding the types of features that enhance program effectiveness. Our own efforts to make such inferences from the 20 programs we review are limited by the narrow range of variation in program features that are likely to matter and the lack of consistency across evaluations in the outcomes that are measured. So although this chapter provides a starting point for answering the "What works?" question, much more remains to be done on this issue.

Outcomes Improved by Early Childhood Intervention Programs

Early childhood interventions may affect participants' outcomes during and immediately after the program, or they may have more-lasting benefits. For participating children, longer-term benefits may be manifested during the school-age years or even in adulthood. In this chapter, we focus on a series of child outcomes that have been evaluated in the 20 programs described in the previous chapter. We first focus on child outcomes that are observed during the schooling years. We then turn to adult outcomes measured at age 18 and beyond. The latter require an evaluation with long-term follow-up, a distinction shared by just five of the 20 programs we analyze.

Outcomes During the School-Age Years

As discussed in Chapter Two, the aim of most early intervention programs is to enhance child development. As such, barometers of program success would include whether children in the program perform better than their control (or comparison) group counterparts on measures of early development and whether those gains are maintained at later ages. Measures of healthy development during the K–12 years include the following domains:

- Cognitive development (includes IQ and achievement test scores)
- Behavioral and emotional development (such as scores on measures of social competence or behavior problems)
- Educational outcomes (special education placement, grade retention, grades, attendance, and others)
- Child maltreatment (includes instances of child abuse)

- Health (injuries, hospital visits, and others)
- Crime (primarily juvenile delinquency and arrests).

In addition to these outcomes, some program evaluations have also collected information about likely precursors to these outcomes. For example, the Reach Out and Read program evaluations examined whether children enjoyed reading and how much parents read to their children in addition to whether measures of children's vocabulary improved (High, Hopmann, et al., 1998; High, LaGasse, et al., 2000). We focus here on the outcomes rather than such precursors.

It is noteworthy that the outcomes the early childhood intervention model stresses—i.e., developmental measures, especially those related to school readiness—are not incorporated into benefit-cost analysis. The first two types of outcomes listed above—cognitive development and behavioral and emotional development—are exceedingly difficult to monetize. Educational outcomes such as special education placement and grade retention are much easier to assign a dollar value to, as are child maltreatment, health, and crime outcomes. Hence, the primary impetus for early childhood intervention is in fact generally outside the scope of the benefit-cost arguments that have been cited so often as justifications for public or wide-scale investments in early childhood. We elaborate on this point in Chapter Four.

Not all of the programs reviewed in this study measured effects in all the domains listed above. In Table 3.1, we list the outcomes that each program measured. A cell with dark shading indicates that a program did not measure the outcome; a light-shaded cell indicates that the outcome was measured but that there was no statistically significant difference between the treatment and control/comparison groups. The remaining cells list the outcomes that were improved by a statistically significant amount compared with a control or comparison group. (Programs are listed according to the taxonomy developed in Chapter Two.) We list an outcome in this table if a significant effect was found in any program evaluation follow-up. For example, if a significant effect was observed at age 5 but not at age 9, the outcome is listed in this table.

Table 3.1
Measured Outcomes and Program Effects for Early Childhood Intervention Evaluations—Child Outcomes

Program	Domain					
	Cognitive/ Achievement	Behavioral/ Emotional	Educational	Child Maltreatment	Health, Accidents, and Injuries	Crime
Home Visiting or Parent Education						
NFP	Achievement test scores	Positive behaviors		Child abuse	Emergency room visits Hospital days	Arrests
DSC/ NIDCAP[a]	Mental indices	Developmental delay			Reflexes Weight gain Hospital stays	
Parents As Teachers[a]	Achievement test scores	Positive behaviors		Child maltreatment	Child health rating Injuries	
Project CARE (no ECE)	///////					
HIPPY USA	Achievement test scores					
Reach Out and Read[a]	Vocabulary					
Dare to Be You	Developmental level	Behavior problems				
Incredible Years		Behavior problems Social competence				
Home Visiting or Parent Education Combined with Early Childhood Education						
Early Head Start[a]	Achievement test scores	Positive behaviors			Child health rating	
Syracuse FDRP	IQ	Positive behaviors	Grades (girls) Attendance (girls) Teacher ratings (girls)			
CCDP	///////	///////	///////			
IHDP	IQ Achievement test scores	Behavior problems	///////		///////	
Project CARE (with ECE)	IQ					
Abecedarian	IQ Achievement test scores		Special education Grade retention			

RAND *MG341-T-3.1a*

Table 3.1—continued

Program	Domain					
	Cognitive/ Achievement	Behavioral/ Emotional	Educational	Child Maltreatment	Health, Accidents, and Injuries	Crime
Home Visiting or Parent Education Combined with Early Childhood Education (continued)						
Houston PCDC	IQ Achievement test scores	Behavior problems				
ETP	IQ Achievement test scores		Special education		Teen pregnancy	
Perry Preschool	IQ Achievement test scores		Special education		Teen pregnancy	Arrests
Chicago CPC	Achievement test scores	Social competence	Special education Grade retention	Child abuse		Delinquency
Head Start	IQ Achievement test scores (mixed)		Grade retention		Immunizations Other positive health behaviors	
Early Childhood Education Only						
Oklahoma Pre-K	Achievement test scores					

☐ Outcome measured and improvement in the listed indicator was statistically significant at the 0.05 level or better.

▨ Outcome measured but difference was not statistically significant at the 0.05 level or better.

▦ Outcome not measured.

SOURCE: Authors' tabulations based on sources cited in Appendix A.

NOTES: See Table 2.2 for full program names and Table 2.3 for program implementation dates and sample sizes.

[a] At the last follow-up, these programs measured outcomes for children as young as age 2 or 3.

Across the programs and outcomes tallied in Table 3.1, when an outcome was measured, a statistically significant favorable effect on participants was found much more frequently than would be expected by chance. For example, six out of seven of the home visiting/parent education programs that measured an outcome in the cognitive and achievement domain found favorable and significant effects, as did 11 of the 12 combination programs. That is, although not every program has an effect in every outcome area, the programs were shown to be successful at improving child outcomes in an overwhelming majority of cases where a measure was collected. Indeed, across all domains listed in Table 3.1, statistically significant benefits were found in at least 70 percent of the programs that measured an outcome in that domain. (Below, we illustrate the same point using more-formal statistical analysis for the cognitive and achievement domain.) It is also worth noting that the consistency in results is based on evaluations of programs implemented in multiple sites such as some of the Head Start or Early Head Start studies. The set of evaluations also includes replications of results for a given program, as is the case for the NFP model (which has been examined in three separate studies in different locations) and the interrelated model evaluated in Abecedarian, Project CARE, and IHDP (which together were studied in 10 locations).

Reflecting the child development objectives of most early intervention programs, most of the program evaluations measured outcomes in the cognitive development domain, and many also measured outcomes related to behavioral and emotional development. Many evaluations examined educational outcomes; fewer evaluations considered child maltreatment, health, and crime outcomes.

The overwhelming majority of the evaluations found that these programs had a favorable and statistically significant effect on children's cognitive development or behavioral and emotional development. The one exception, CCDP, found favorable effects, though with only marginal statistical significance. Notably, this lack of a significant finding has been attributed to the methodological concerns with the program evaluation discussed in Chapter Two. Another exception, the Project CARE model with no ECE, found an unfavorable effect on IQ, although it was not statistically significant. The most frequently measured outcomes related to development were IQ test scores, achievement test scores, and measures of social competence or behavior problems.

Of those programs that assessed the educational performance of participants, most also observed better outcomes for program participants than for their counterparts in the comparison group. The most common measures of school performance were special education placement and grade retention. Finally, when evaluations measured outcomes in the other domains, programs were also found to have a favorable effect. An important footnote in terms of "what we know" about the effects of early childhood intervention is that many evaluations did not measure outcomes in the domains of health, child maltreatment and crime.

Outcomes in Adulthood

Five of the 20 programs we examine have followed program participants long enough for us to know something about the longer-term effects of early childhood programs. Table 3.2 reports the findings from these studies with respect to four domains: educational attainment, employment and earnings, social services use, and crime. Outcomes in these domains have been measured from age 18 up to age 40. We follow the same approach adopted in Table 3.1 in terms of which favorable outcomes are represented in the table and how the cells are shaded. All five programs use the combination program approach.

For the four outcome domains, we again observe that when programs measured an outcome, they were more likely to find a favorable and significant effect than one would expect due to chance. At least two-thirds of studies measuring an outcome found a significant effect in all domains except social services use (where only one of two programs that measured this outcome found a significant effect). Of the five programs, only the ETP failed to find any statistically significant long-term effects, and it had one of the smallest sample sizes. A consistent finding for the four other studies is that the intervention

Table 3.2
Measured Outcomes and Program Effects for Early Childhood Intervention Evaluations—Adult Outcomes

Program	Adult Outcome Domain			
	Educational Attainment	Employment and Earnings	Social Services Use	Crime
Home Visiting or Parent Education Combined with Early Childhood Education				
Abecedarian	Years of completed schooling Ever attended four-year college	Skilled employment	▨	▨
ETP	▨	▩	▩	▩
Perry Preschool	High school graduation	Employment Earnings Income	Use of social services	Arrests Arrests for violent crimes Time in prison/jail
Chicago CPC	High school graduation Highest grade completed	▩	▩	Arrests Arrests for violent crimes
Head Start	High school graduation (whites) College attendance (whites)	▨	▩	Booked or charged with crime (blacks)

☐ Outcome measured and improvement in the listed indicator was statistically significant at the 0.05 level or better.

▨ Outcome measured but difference was not statistically significant at the 0.05 level or better.

▩ Outcome not measured.

SOURCE: Authors' tabulations based on sources cited in Appendix A.

NOTES: See Table 2.2 for full program names and Table 2.3 for program implementation dates and sample sizes.

RAND MG341-T-3.2

increased rates of high school graduation or years of schooling completed. College attendance has also been favorably affected. Improved labor market outcomes include higher employment rates, higher rates of employment in skilled jobs, and increased earnings. The Perry Preschool program found a concomitant decrease in reliance on welfare or other social services programs. Finally, three of the four programs that measured contact with the criminal justice system show a favorable effect.

Magnitude of the Effects

While statistical analysis might designate an effect as "significant" because we can have a high degree of confidence that it is not zero, it is another matter to assess whether the effect is meaningful in terms of size. Evaluations of early childhood interventions necessarily use prevailing statistical standards to designate program effects as "significant" or "insignificant." In this section, we focus on putting these program effects into context in terms of their magnitude.

To compare the magnitude of different program effects, program effects are typically converted to a standardized measure called *effect size*.[1] For example, how does one compare the size of the reduction in juvenile arrests realized in one program with the increase in scores on an achievement test gained in another program? The effect size is generally calculated by dividing the program effect measure by the standard deviation of that effect measure. In an experimental evaluation, the effect measure would be the difference in the outcomes of the treatment and control groups. This effect measure is divided by the standard deviation of the outcome for treatment and control groups combined to get the effect size. In other words, the magnitude of the effect is standardized by a measure of the spread of the outcome. An effect size of 0.30 would correspond to a treatment group mean that is 0.30 standard deviations above the control group mean. In terms of a standard normal distribution, this would imply that the mean treatment group outcome is better than the outcomes of 62 percent of the control group, whereas if there were no effect the

---

[1] Another way to put program effects into perspective is to compare them with those from other types of interventions. For example, approaches to improving elementary-age children's achievement scores might range from enriched preschool programs to reducing class size or raising the minimum kindergarten entry age. Chapter Four discusses in detail another way to compare program effects—benefit-cost analysis—which expresses outcomes in dollar terms so that they can be aggregated and compared with program costs.

mean of the treatment group would be only better than 50 percent of the control group. We estimate an *adjusted effect size*, which accounts for potential biases arising from small sample sizes, as described in more detail in Appendix B.

While no "industry standard" exists regarding what constitutes a meaningful program effect size, several noted authors have suggested conventions while acknowledging that the concept of effect size is subjective. For example, Crane (1998) considers an effect size of more than 0.25 to be large. Cohen (1988) designates an effect size of 0.20 as "small," one of 0.50 as "medium," and one of 0.80 as "large."

We note that, given the differences in evaluation methodologies discussed in Chapter Two, the effect sizes we consider in this section may not be strictly comparable. For example, the program effects and the associated effect sizes from quasi-experimental designs are more likely to be biased upward if the evaluation design did not fully correct for possible selection bias in the treatment group. On the other hand, the methodological concerns about the CCDP evaluation have been suggested as an explanation for a possible downward bias in that program's estimated effects and therefore for the associated effect sizes. The differences in the services received by the control group (the baseline services) may also contribute to differences in estimated effect sizes. Moreover, it can be problematic to compare effect sizes across different outcome measures because some outcomes are more amenable to change, thereby making it easier to generate larger effect sizes for a given intervention.

Despite these caveats, we feel it is instructive to use the estimated effect sizes for the 20 programs we identified as a way to assess the overall magnitude of early intervention program effects, rather than as a mechanism for suggesting that some programs are necessarily more effective than others because their effect sizes are larger. In our discussion, we focus on effect sizes within outcome domains for measures that are as comparable as possible (e.g., achievement test scores or measures of grade repetition). We begin by examining the magnitudes of outcomes for younger children, followed by those for older children and adults and for other program participants.

Cognitive Outcomes for Younger Children

Cognitive outcomes were the most frequently measured among the 20 programs we feature in this study. Out of 20 evaluations, 16 report an achievement test score, an IQ score, or both, and have sufficient information available to calculate the effect size.[2] The estimated effect sizes for an achievement test score at approximately ages 5 to 6, closest to the age of school entry, are shown in Figure 3.1.[3] In one case, Houston PCDC, the test score is only available at 9.5 years of age. Because programs in the "promising" category have not followed children into the school-age years, we used the achievement test score at the oldest age available, which was generally around age 3. Again, the early intervention programs are ordered by the taxonomy developed in Chapter Two.

As seen in Figure 3.1, all but two of the effect sizes are positive, meaning that the program improved cognitive outcomes. The two negative scores were statistically insignificant. The largest effect size measured was 0.97 (significant at the 0.01 level), which was found for the Stanford-Binet test administered to the Perry Preschool evaluation participants at age 5. The second largest effect size is found for the Letter-Word Identification Subtest of the Woodcock-Johnson Achievement Test among participants in the Oklahoma Pre-K pro-

---

[2] Although the Syracuse FDRP reported the program effect on IQ, the study did not report sufficient information to calculate the corresponding effect size (Honig and Lally, 1982). Likewise, it was not possible to calculate the corresponding effect size for the achievement test score effect reported by Currie and Thomas (1995) for Head Start. Two other programs—DSC/NIDCAP and Incredible Years—did not report either an achievement test or IQ score program effect.

[3] If a general achievement test score was available, we used that (including, for example, the assessment of the level of child development measured in DARE to be You). When only subject-specific scores were available, we used the reading score. If no achievement score was available, we used an IQ score. For programs that reported analyses of multiple samples, we pooled the samples. For example, the Houston PCDC study reports results separately for boys and girls, and we pool these (Johnson and Walker, 1991). Similarly, we pool the two cohorts of the HIPPY evaluations. Due to these selection criteria regarding the cognitive outcome measure to report in Figure 3.1, the statistical significance of the specific measure recorded in Figure 3.1 may be different from the result reported in Table 3.1. In other words, while the measure reported in Figure 3.1 may be statistically insignificant at the 5-percent level, another test score measure at the same age or another age may have been statistically significant at that level. Hence the designation in Table 3.1.

Figure 3.1
Cognitive Outcome Effect Sizes Near or in Elementary School

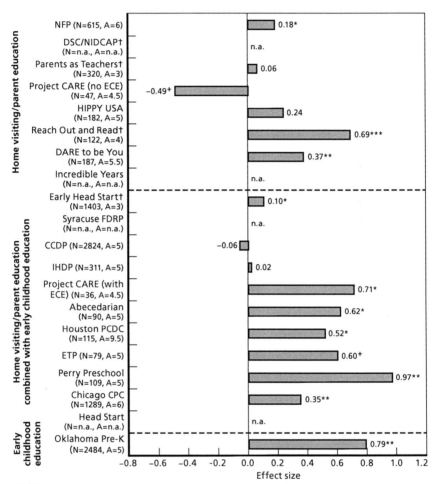

SOURCE: Authors' tabulations based on sources cited in Appendix A.

NOTES: See Table 2.2 for full program names and Table 2.3 for program evaluation dates. Programs with an dagger are designated as having a promising evidence base. Other programs are designated as having a strong evidence base. The effect size is based on general achievement test scores when available, or reading achievement scores or IQ results. Numbers in parentheses after program names indicate total sample size (N) and age of measurement (A).

$+$ p < 0.10; * p < 0.05; ** p < 0.01; *** p < 0.001.

n.a. = not applicable or not available.

RAND MG341-3.1

gram. Gormley et al. (forthcoming) report that this is equivalent to a gain in age-equivalent scores of approximately seven to eight months.

Both of these effect sizes, as well as several others shown in Figure 3.1, would be considered large by the standards of educational interventions. Looking across the programs by our taxonomy, the effect sizes for the home visiting and parent education programs range from –0.49 to 0.69, with a mean of 0.17. The negative effect size for the Project CARE program without ECE and the near-zero effect size for Parents as Teachers clearly lower the mean substantially from what it would have been without these two programs. The effect sizes for the combination programs range from near zero to 0.97, with a mean of 0.43. In this case, the mean effect size would be larger if Early Head Start, CCDP, and IHDP had been excluded.

We also conducted a more formal meta-analysis of these effect sizes to test whether the mean effect size of these programs was in fact different from zero. We estimated the pooled mean effect size for cognitive outcomes across all programs shown in Figure 3.1.[4] This effect size estimate, which accounts for differences in the distributions of the different studies in the sample, is 0.28, and we could reject the hypothesis that this estimate was zero with a high degree of confidence ($p = 0.000$). In other words, the statistical analysis affirms that the effect size of about 0.3 is significantly different from zero, indicating that these programs on average do have a small-to-moderate positive effect on cognitive outcomes at about the time of school entry.[5]

For achievement test scores, Table 3.3 shows the results from the Chicago CPC evaluations as the children in this study grew older. Children who attended the CPC program and comparison children were assessed in reading and math using the Iowa Test of Basic Skills in grades 3, 5, and 8. CPC children outscored their comparison group counterparts in each year, with effect sizes ranging from 0.17

[4] A test of homogeneity of the study distributions was rejected at the $p = 0.000$ level.

[5] These findings do not change when we exclude the CCDP results from the analysis because of the potential methodological concerns discussed in Chapter Two.

Table 3.3
Achievement Test Effect Sizes for the Chicago CPC Program

Outcome	N	Treatment	Comparison	Difference	Effect Size
Reading achievement score by grade					
Third grade	1,289	98.6	92.9	5.7***	0.34
Fifth grade	1,234	112.8	109.8	3.0**	0.17
Eighth grade	1,158	146.1	142.3	3.8	0.17
Math achievement score by grade					
Third grade	1,289	101.8	97.6	4.2***	0.32
Fifth grade	1,234	118.5	114.7	3.8***	0.24
Eighth grade	1,158	148.4	144.9	3.5**	0.19

SOURCE: Reynolds (1997), Table 5.
NOTES: Achievement test score is the Iowa Test of Basic Skills standard score. N = sample size for combined treatment and control groups. The final column shows the mean difference effect size estimated using the standard mean difference effect size for continuous variables (see Lipsey and Wilson, 2001, Appendix B).
* $p<0.05$, ** $p<0.01$, *** $p<0.001$.

to 0.34 (Reynolds, 1997). Although designating effect sizes is subjective, these effect sizes would be considered small to moderate using either of the standards mentioned above. Another way to put these results in perspective is to note that these differences are about one-sixth to one-third of a standard deviation.

These results illustrate two other key points. First, they show that the gains from early childhood intervention programs are certainly meaningful but often are not necessarily so large that they fully compensate for the disadvantages faced by the at-risk population served by the intervention. In other words, although the treated children outperform the comparison group children, the gains are not so large that the children's outcomes match those of children who are not from disadvantaged backgrounds.

Second, these achievement scores exhibit a phenomenon observed in a number of early childhood evaluations: fade-out. That is, the differences in scores between the treatment and comparison groups get smaller over time, and in some cases become insignificant.

Using data from 33 early childhood programs, Aos et al. (2004) find a consistent pattern of fade-out in the test score advantage for treated children over time. Similar patterns have been observed in other individual programs (e.g., Perry Preschool), although the Abecedarian program—arguably the most intensive of those we examine—provides one exception: The IQ and achievement test score advantage for program participants persisted through age 21 (Karoly et al., 1998; Campbell et al., 2002). Nevertheless, as is evident from Tables 3.1 and 3.2 and as we discuss further below, while there may be fade-out in the effect of early childhood interventions on IQ or achievement test scores for most programs, there is evidence of lasting benefits in other aspects of educational attainment and subsequent economic outcomes in adulthood.

There is speculation that the gains realized in the programs may not be maintained as children get older unless some type of intervention is maintained over time or unless children continue to receive high-quality educational services (see the discussion in Blau and Currie, 2004). Indeed, the continued services offered in the Abecedarian program from kindergarten through age 8 and in the Chicago CPC program from kindergarten through third grade have been demonstrated to confer added benefits beyond those obtained from the preschool intervention (Campbell and Ramey, 1995; Reynolds, 2000). Likewise, in their meta-analysis of longitudinal research on preschool programs, Nelson, Westhues, and MacLeod (2003) find that programs with a follow-on component in elementary school have larger effects on cognitive outcomes for elementary-age children.

Because designating effect sizes as large or small is subjective, it can be instructive to compare the effect sizes of one type of intervention with effect sizes from another type of intervention. To put the effect sizes of early intervention programs into perspective, we provide a few examples of the effect sizes found from studies that examined the effect of other interventions on test scores. In an evaluation of a program in which elementary-age students directly teach, supervise, and evaluate their peers' performance, Greenwood (1991) found effect sizes of 0.37, 0.57, and 0.60 for math, reading, and language achievement, respectively. Greenwood's evaluation of Classwide Peer

Tutoring (CWPT) measured gains on fourth grade achievement tests of low-SES students who had participated in CWPT since first grade.

Another example comes from Project STAR, Tennessee's class-size reduction experiment. Kindergarten students within the same schools were randomly assigned to a small class (13–17 students), a larger class (22–26 students), or a larger class with a full-time teacher's aide. Nearly 12,000 students were evaluated by the end of the third grade (Finn and Achilles, 1999). The effect sizes by the third grade were 0.25 for a measure of language skills, 0.26 in reading, and 0.23 in mathematics.

Other Outcomes for School-Age Children

Fewer programs measured outcomes related to behavioral, emotional, and social outcomes, as shown in Table 3.1. Nevertheless, ten out of the twelve programs that measured a behavioral or social outcome had a statistically significant effect on at least one measure in this area. The measures collected in this domain range from assessments of behavior problems and aggression to measures of life skills. As such, favorable results for these outcomes are sometimes manifested as a negative effect (i.e., the control group mean exceeds the treatment group mean)—such as when the measure captures behavior problems—and sometimes as a positive effect.

In terms of the magnitudes of the effects, outcomes in the social and behavioral domain tend to exhibit effect sizes that are not as large as those for the cognitive outcomes. In Table 3.4, we list several illustrative behavioral and social measures assessed at age 5 or older and their estimated effect sizes.[6] When statistically significant, the effect sizes are in the moderate range (e.g., 0.3), and they can persist to older ages such as the statistically significant favorable life skills meas-

---

[6] Again, there may be differences in the statistical significance of measures recorded in Table 3.4 and the summary designation in Table 3.1. Table 3.1 reflects whether any measure in the behavioral/emotional domain was statistically significant for a given program; Table 3.4 shows several illustrative measures at age 5 or older, not necessarily those that were statistically significant for the programs shown.

Table 3.4
Social and Behavioral Outcome Effect Sizes for Early Childhood Intervention Programs

Outcome	N	Treatment	Comparison	Difference	Effect Size
Home Visiting or Parent Education					
Aggression measure: NFP, age 6, low psychological resource mothers	335	98.6	101.1	−2.5*	−0.25
Problem behavior measure: DARE to be You, ages 9–13	187	16.4	17.9	−1.5	−0.12
Home Visiting or Parent Education Combined with Early Childhood Education					
Child behavior checklist (total problems): IHDP, age 5	865	31.9	33.0	−1.1	−0.06
Life skills measure: Chicago CPC, grade 8	115	40.7	37.7	3.0***	0.28

SOURCE: NFP: Olds, Kitzman, et al. (2004), Table 4; DARE to be You: Miller-Heyl, MacPhee, and Fritz, (1998), Table 4; IHDP: Brooks-Gunn et al. (1994), Table 2; CPC: Reynolds (1997), Table 6.

NOTES: See Table 2.2 for full program names. Life skills measure is the Minimum Proficiency Skills Test. Aggression measure is based on McArthur Story Stem Battery. N = sample size for combined treatment and control groups. The final column shows the mean difference effect size estimated using the standard mean difference effect size for continuous variables (see Lipsey and Wilson, 2001, Appendix B).

* $p < 0.05$, ** $p < 0.01$, *** $p < 0.001$.

ure assessed in eighth grade as part of the Chicago CPC evaluation. In general, the outcomes in this domain do not produce effect sizes that match some of the larger effects evident for cognitive outcomes seen in Figure 3.1.

Although the magnitude of effects for either the cognitive measures or social and behavioral measures may not seem large, it is not clear how changes in these measures correspond to changes in other outcomes. For example, it could be that a small change in problem behavior is associated with greater school attendance as well as improved attention while in school, resulting in a lower chance of grade repetition. Early intervention programs have larger effects on some of the other outcomes, such as those related to educational progress and attainment.

For example, Table 3.5 shows the estimated effect sizes associated with special education placement and grade retention in four programs that measured these outcomes (all combination programs).[7] These outcomes are typically expressed as the percentage of a group that has ever been retained in grade or ever been in special education classes during all or most of the K–12 years, although sometimes the measure is the number of years repeated or in special education. The effect sizes for these outcomes, measured at older ages, are generally greater in magnitude than the effects found for behavioral assessments, and they are as large as or larger than those for cognitive outcomes at older ages (when fade-out typically sets in). For instance, the age-15 evaluation of the Carolina Abecedarian Project found that 24.5 percent of the program children had been in special education classes by that age compared with 47.7 percent of the control group children (Campbell and Ramey, 1995). This difference of 23.2 percentage points corresponds to an absolute effect size of 0.49. Similarly, by age 15, the children in the Abecedarian program were substantially less likely to have been retained in grade than the comparison group children were, with a nearly equivalent effect size. Two of the effects in Table 3.5 for grade retention are not significant (the one for ETP is in the wrong direction), but the remaining effects range from about one-quarter to three-quarters of a standard deviation.

Many of the measured effects for the remaining types of outcomes listed in Table 3.1 are also sizable. For example, among higher-

---

[7] Grade repetition and use of special education were also measured in the Houston PCDC study, but the difference between the treatment and control groups for both outcomes were statistically insignificant. Currie and Thomas (1995) also examine grade repetition in their quasi-experimental analysis of Head Start and find significant effects for white children. The results from their regression-based analysis do not readily translate into the treatment-control group differences reported in Table 3.5.

Table 3.5
Special Education Placement and Grade Retention Effect Sizes for Early
Childhood Intervention Programs

Outcome	N	Treatment	Comparison	Difference	Effect Size
Home Visiting or Parent Education Combined with Early Childhood Education					
Grade retention					
Abecedarian (by age 15) (%)	92	31.2	54.5	−23.3*	−0.48
ETP (by age 18) (%)	62	58.5	52.4	6.2	0.12
Perry Preschool (by age 27) (years)	112	0.5	0.7	−0.2	−0.15
Chicago CPC (by age 15) (%)	1,281	23.0	38.4	−15.4***	−0.34
Special education					
Abecedarian (by age 15) (%)	92	24.5	47.7	−23.2*	−0.49
ETP (by age 18) (%)	62	4.9	33.3	−28.5***	−0.79
Perry Preschool (by age 19) (% of years)	112	16	28	−12*	−0.29
Chicago CPC (by age 18) (%)	1,281	14.4	24.6	−10.2***	−0.26

SOURCE: Chicago CPC Program: Reynolds et al. (2002), Table 4 and authors' calculations (for effect sizes); ETP: Gray, Ramsey, and Klaus (1983), Table 2.4, and authors'
calculations (for effect sizes); Perry Preschool: Berrueta-Clement et al. (1984), Table
6, and Schweinhart, Barnes, and Weikart (1993), Table 10, and authors' calculations
(for effect sizes); Carolina Abecedarian: Campbell and Ramey (1995), in text, and
authors' calculations (for effect sizes).
NOTES: See Table 2.2 for full program names. N is sample size for combined treatment and control groups. The final column shows the mean difference effect size
estimated using the arcsine transformation of the difference between two proportions for dichotomous outcomes and as the standard mean difference effect size for
continuous variables (see Lipsey and Wilson, 2001, Appendix B).
* $p < 0.05$, ** $p < 0.01$, *** $p < 0.001$.

risk families in the Elmira, New York trial, the NFP program found a
reduction in emergency room visits between 25 and 50 months of age
for about one-third of participants compared with the control group

(Olds, Henderson, and Kitzman, 1994) and a reduction of more than one-half in the number of arrests by age 15 for participants compared with the control group (Olds, Eckenrode, et al., 1997). It is interesting to note that in a recent follow-up study of the NFP, the authors calculated effect sizes for a large set of differences in mean child outcomes for the children receiving the program compared with the control group. These effect sizes range in magnitude from 0.02 to 0.34 (Olds, Kitzman, et al., 2004, Table 4.).

Longer-Term Outcomes and Effects for Other Program Participants

The magnitudes associated with the favorable effects of early childhood interventions on adult outcomes can also be sizable. Table 3.6 features these findings, again for the subset of programs with long-term evaluations (all of them combination programs).[8] The absolute effect sizes for the statistically significant outcomes range from about 0.2 to 0.5, similar to the range noted for grade repetition and special education use.[9] These figures for the longer-term effects of early childhood programs, as well as the evidence for educational measures seen in Table 3.5, point to the potential of early childhood

---

[8] We do not report results for Head Start because the quasi-experimental results reported by Garces, Thomas, and Currie (2002) do not readily translate into treatment-control group differences and effect sizes. For the Perry Preschool program, we report effects and effect sizes based on results as of the age-27 follow-up (Schweinhart, Barnes, and Weikart, 1993) as well as the age-40 follow-up (Schweinhart et al., 2005). Although the measures of high school completion, crime, and earnings were significant at both ages for Perry Preschool, the measure of employment was significant only at age 40 and the measure of social services use was significant only at age 27.

[9] In some cases, consistent with the results reported in Table 3.2, the outcomes reported in Table 3.6 are not significant. For example, Abecedarian did not find a significant effect on high school graduation rates by age 21. However, program participants had more years of completed schooling (12.2 years for the treatment group compared with 11.6 years for the control group, p < 0.05) and were more likely to have attended a four-year college (36 percent for the treatment group compared with 14 percent for the control group, p < 0.01) (Campbell et al., 2002). Although the employment rate was not statistically significant in Abecedarian, there was a significant difference in the fraction with a skilled job as measured by the Hollingshead scale. None of the crime outcomes measured in Abecedarian was statistically significant. Results for felony convictions are shown in Table 3.6, but there was also no effect for misdemeanor convictions or incarcerations. ETP did not find a significant effect for high school graduation rates, the only long-term outcome it measured in the domains shown in Table 3.2.

interventions for long-lasting benefits. An important feature of the outcomes in domains other than the cognitive and behavioral is that, in addition to being larger in magnitude, they also persist long after any cognitive advantage has diminished. In other words, although the test score advantage realized by program participants may shrink over time to the point of no longer being significant, most of the other gains accruing to program participants are maintained over the longer term—even as late as age 40, as evident in the results for Perry Preschool.[10] As we will see in Chapter Four, many of these long-term benefits provide the basis for valuing the economic returns from early interventions so that they can be compared with program costs.

In addition to improving outcomes for participating children, early childhood intervention programs may improve outcomes for their parents, typically the mother of the child (since many at-risk children are in mother-only households). Although fewer evaluations have examined this possibility, the existing evidence supports the idea that parents as well as children can realize substantial benefits. Studies have found that participating mothers exhibit improved parenting skills, greater educational attainment and employment, reduced use of public assistance, more positive health behaviors, and less criminal activity (see Karoly et al., 1998, and Brooks-Gunn, Berlin, and Fuligni, 2000, for summaries). Of the 20 programs included in this study, 15 measured outcomes for mothers, although seven of them measured outcomes related only to parenting skills. In three of the 15 programs, none of the measures was statistically significant; the others all had one or more significant changes in parental outcomes. As with the outcomes for participating children, the effect sizes for maternal outcomes also tend to be in the small-to-moderate range. However, as we discuss in Chapter Four, even small changes in maternal outcomes

_____

[10] As seen in Table 3.6, the measure of social welfare program use in the age-40 Perry Preschool follow-up is no longer statistically significant, whereas a related measure at age 27 was significant. The other outcomes shown in Table 3.6 remained statistically significant at age 40. A direct comparison of the magnitudes of the effects at ages 27 and 40 is not always possible, however, because the measures are not always the same.

Table 3.6
Long-Term Effects for Early Childhood Intervention Programs

Outcome	N	Treatment	Comparison	Difference	Effect Size
Home Visiting or Parent Education Combined with Early Childhood Education					
High school completion					
Abecedarian (by age 21) (%)	104	70	67	3	0.06
ETP (by age 18) (%)	62	61.0	47.6	13.4	0.27
Perry Preschool (by age 27) (%)	123	66	45	21*	0.43
Perry Preschool (by age 40) (%)	119	77	60	17*	0.37
Chicago CPC (by age 20) (%)	1,233	49.7	38.5	11.2**	0.23
Adult crime and delinquency					
Abecedarian (by age 21) (% with felony conviction)	104	8	12	−4	0.13
Perry Preschool (by age 27) (# of arrests)	123	2.3	4.6	−2.3**	−0.54
Perry Preschool (by age 40) (% with one or more arrests)	n.a.	71	83	−12*	−0.29
Chicago CPC (by age 18) (% with petitions to juvenile court)	1,404	16.9	25.1	−8.2**	−0.20
Chicago CPC (by age 18) (% with petitions to juvenile court for violent offense)	1,404	9.0	15.3	−6.3**	−0.19
Employment and earnings					
Abecedarian (at age 21) (% employed)	104	64	50	14	0.28
Abecedarian (at age 21) (% skilled jobs)	104	67	41	23**	0.53
Perry Preschool (at age 27) (% employed)	116	71	59	12	0.25

Table 3.6—continued

Outcome	N	Treatment	Comparison	Difference	Effect Size
Perry Preschool (at age 40) (% employed)	112	76	62	14*	0.30
Perry Preschool (at age 27) (monthly earnings $1,993)	115	1219	766	453**	0.51
Perry Preschool (at age 40) (median monthly earnings)	112	1,856	1,308	548[a]	n.a.
Social services use (welfare, food stamps, etc.)					
Abecedarian (at age 21) (% current participation)	104	8	16	–8	–0.25
Perry Preschool (by age 27) (% received in past 10 years)	123	59	80	–21**	0.44
Perry Preschool (by age 40) (% any lifetime use of social services)	n.a.	71	86	–15	–0.37

SOURCE: Carolina Abecedarian: Campbell et al. (2002), Masse and Barnett (2002), and authors' calculations (for effect sizes); CPC: Reynolds et al. (2002), Table 4 and author's calculations (for effect sizes); Early Training Project: Gray, Ramsey, and Klaus (1983), Table 2.4, and authors' calculations (for effect sizes); and Perry Preschool: Schweinhart, Barnes, and Weikart (1993), Tables 9, 18, 22, and 24, Schweinhart et al. (2005), Tables 3.1, 4.1, 4.3, and 5.1, and author's calculations (for effect sizes).

NOTES: See Table 2.2 for full program names. N is sample size for combined treatment and control groups. The final column shows the mean difference effect size estimated using the arcsine transformation of the difference between two proportions for dichotomous outcomes and as the standard mean difference effect size for continuous variables (see Lipsey and Wilson, 2001, Appendix B). Perry Preschool statistical tests at age 40 are based on one-tailed tests. n.a. = not available.

* p < 0.05, ** p < 0.01, *** p < 0.001.

[a] A statistical test for the difference in median earnings is not reported but a test of the difference in the distribution of earnings is statistically significant at the 5-percent level based on a 1-tailed test.

can produce large savings for the government and add to the favorable benefit-cost ratios for these programs.

In addition to the evidence we present here, several recent meta-analyses have examined the range of effect sizes for early childhood programs. In a review of home visiting programs, Sweet and Appelbaum (2004) found effect sizes ranging from –0.043 to 0.318. They also found that home visiting programs consistently improved six of ten mother and child outcomes. Also consistent with the summary of effect sizes above, Aos et al. (2004) found effect sizes ranging from 0.13 to 0.18 for outcomes before the end of high school based on a meta-analysis of early childhood education and home visiting programs serving primarily disadvantaged children. Finally, Nelson, Westhues, and MacLeod (2003) conducted a meta-analysis of 34 preschool prevention programs for disadvantaged children using inclusion criteria different from those we use in this study. The primary differences are that Nelson et al. admitted studies with smaller sample sizes and those with nonrandom assignment to the treatment groups. They measured a mean effect size of 0.30 for cognitive outcomes from kindergarten through eighth grade, with similar effect sizes for socioemotional outcomes and parent-family wellness outcomes.

In sum, the early childhood intervention programs reviewed in this study demonstrate that such programs can have a statistically significant effect on a range of outcomes, both early in children's educational careers and later into adolescence and adulthood. The size of these effects for cognitive and behavioral measures is relatively modest, and these gains may fade as children age. However, the magnitude can be substantial for some of the other outcomes, such as special education placement, grade retention, and criminal activity. Moreover, there is evidence that the advantage realized by program participants in these areas can be maintained over the longer term as children transition to adulthood. As we will see in Chapter Four, the latter outcomes are also those that are most easily monetized as part of a benefit-cost analysis.

Features Associated with More-Effective Programs

Our summary of what contributes to the effectiveness of early childhood programs draws on two sources of information. First, numerous research studies have had as their central research question the issue of what aspects of these programs improve children's outcomes. For example, David Olds and his colleagues have explored whether outcomes from home visiting programs are better when nurses or social workers provide the services. Second, we review prior studies and conduct original analysis to determine whether program intensity and type appear to be associated with greater program effectiveness.

Studies of Program Characteristics

Research that has tried to get "inside the black box" to examine what features of early childhood intervention programs are associated with greater effectiveness has examined two types of characteristics. The first is structural characteristics—those that can be counted or quantified in a relatively straightforward way. They include such features as staff education or child-to-staff ratios. The second type is "process" characteristics. These are less tangible features, such as the nature of caregiver interactions with children (see Love, Schochet, and Meckstroth, 1996, and Hayes, Palmer, and Zaslow, 1990, for discussions of structural and process quality for child care). Examples of the types of caregiver interactions examined include the warmth of caregivers, responsiveness of caregivers, and the level of involvement of the caregivers.

A number of expert panel reports and review articles have made recommendations regarding the quality standards and characteristics that early childhood programs should maintain (for example, Behrman, Gomby, and Culross, 1999; Brooks-Gunn, Berlin, and Fuligni, 2000; and Board on Children, Youth, and Families, 2001). There are fewer evidence-based references that provide guidance on these issues. None of the studies of process quality meet the criteria for rigorous research methodology employed by this study to select programs for inclusion in the analysis and in-depth discussion. Specifically, the majority of these studies used relatively weak nonexperimental study designs that do not convincingly control for potential differences between treatment and comparison groups.[11]

---

[11] We do not discuss this research here, but readers can find more information about studies of process quality in Blau and Currie (2004) and Vandell and Wolfe (2000).

The overwhelming majority of studies of structural quality are also fraught with methodological shortcomings. However, several studies stand out because the researchers were able to conduct experimental evaluations of measures of structural quality. The National Day Care Study (Ruopp et al., 1979) randomly assigned three- and four-year-old children to 29 child care settings that varied in their caregiver education and child-to-staff ratios. They compared the gains in outcomes of children over a nine-month period on a range of outcomes and examined three caregiver education levels—bachelor's degree or greater, associate's degree, or less than an associate's degree—and two child-to-staff ratios—7:1 and 4:1. Although the gains of children with more-educated providers and smaller classes did not outpace other children on every outcome measure, there was evidence that "better" quality was associated with gains for a number of outcomes. Children in smaller classes outperformed their peers on measures of gains in cooperative behavior, hostility and conflict, verbal initiation, receptive language, and general knowledge. Children with more-educated caregivers also made greater gains in the area of cooperative behavior, as well as task persistence and a measure of school readiness.

A second study of structural quality that employed an experimental design also focused on differences in staff education. Two evaluations of the NFP program compared maternal and child outcomes when the program was implemented by paraprofessionals versus nurses to assess whether the type of professional training of the home visitor affected the outcomes. The first evaluation (Olds et al., 2002) compared the maternal and child outcomes up to two years after the intervention for the two types of visitors with a control group. They found that the outcomes for the control group and the group visited by paraprofessionals were not statistically different for a wide range of outcomes assessed. There was one exception: Mother-child pairs in which the mother had low psychological resources and were visited by paraprofessionals interacted with each other more responsively. In contrast, the nurse-visited mother-child pairs realized significantly better outcomes than the control group on maternal outcomes and child outcomes, including fewer language delays and superior mental development at 24 months. A subsequent follow-up when the children were four years old (Olds, Robinson, et al., 2004) found that women visited by paraprofessionals had experienced better outcomes than their control counterparts by this time, but their children were not different from the control children. The nurse-visited mothers and children continued to benefit from the program relative to the control group, with the children scoring better on measures of early learning, language development, executive functioning, and behavioral adaptation. In sum, these evaluations indicate that this home visiting program yielded better outcomes for children when nurses delivered the services.

In a study using quasi-experimental econometric analysis, Currie and Neidell (forthcoming) find evidence from data on Head Start participants consistent with these studies. For children older than 60 months, the results indicate that greater spending on Head Start is associated with higher subsequent reading scores and lower grade retention. Holding per capita expenditures constant, Currie and Neidell find that children in programs with higher teacher-pupil ratios outscore other children, while the fraction of qualified teachers, teachers' salaries, teacher degrees and experience, and characteristics of the directors are not related to children's outcomes.

In addition to program staff characteristics and staff-child ratios, other studies consider the effect of specific program services or the intensity of services. The Project CARE evaluation compared the efficacy of intensive child-care center attendance coupled with home-based parent training (which we categorize in the combination program group) to parent training alone (which we call Project CARE with no ECE) and to a control group that received neither of those treatments (Ramey et al., 1985; Wasik et al., 1990). At assessments conducted as the study children aged from 6 to 54 months, the evaluation found that the group that received early education plus parent training outscored the other two groups on cognitive measures, but there was no significant difference between the group that received parent training only and the control group.

Researchers have also used differences in intensity of participation among participants in the IHDP to examine the possibility that higher levels of participation produce better outcomes. Hill, Brooks-Gunn, and Waldfogel (2003) combine experimental and nonexperimental methods to compare outcomes for infants who attended more than 400 days of the program to those who attended less than 400 days. At age 8, the higher-intensity respondents scored between seven and ten points higher on a cognitive test with a mean of about 90, indicating that effects were larger for higher treatment intensity but also were sustained to older ages.

Analysis of Model Program Evaluations

A second approach to identifying which characteristics improve program effectiveness is to pool the information on well-evaluated programs and examine their characteristics. A recent meta-analysis summarized the evidence related to home visiting (Sweet and Appelbaum, 2004). This study included data from 60 home visiting programs. Their inclusion criteria were designed to include the widest range of information on home visiting programs rather than being limited to those with the most rigorous evaluations. This study found that home visiting programs consistently improved six of ten mother and child outcomes. For each of these ten outcomes, Sweet and Appelbaum explored the relationship between program characteristics and program effect. The program characteristics they examined included design features, such as home visitor staff type and child age at intervention, population targeted, and primary goal. They found no consistent pattern across outcome groups in terms of which program characteristics were associated with greater success. This study was limited, however, by the fact that there is little variation in some of the characteristics across programs. For example, most home visiting programs begin the intervention at about the same age of the child and have similar program goals.

In analysis similar to our analysis presented below, Nelson et al. (2003) also aim to identify program characteristics associated with program success in their meta-analysis of preschool prevention programs. They find a larger average effect size on cognitive outcomes in elementary-age children for early intervention programs with an educational component compared with programs not having one (0.30

versus 0.22), but the difference is not statistically significant. However, they do report a larger average statistically significant effect size on cognitive outcomes measured in the preschool period for early childhood programs with an educational component compared with those not having one (0.53 compared to 0.09). They find greater K–8 socioemotional outcomes for programs with an intervention length greater than one year, but this result does not hold true for K–8 cognitive outcomes. Similarly, for K–8 parent-family outcomes, they report better outcomes for programs consisting of more than 300 sessions, but again they do not find this result for cognitive outcomes.

Drawing on results from the 20 programs included in this study, we examine the relationship between program characteristics and the most commonly reported outcome: scores on cognitive assessments as shown in Figure 3.1. We could not analyze other outcomes because not enough studies measured the outcomes and there was not enough variation in the characteristics of programs evaluated in the studies that reported these outcomes. For example, we considered examining whether a program focused on the mother or child. However, we could not distinguish among programs on this dimension simultaneously with the program type because early childhood education programs typically focus on the child, whereas home visiting or parent training programs typically focus on the parent.

Our analysis focuses on comparing the mean effect sizes for the 19 programs included in two of the approaches used in the taxonomy introduced in Chapter Two: home visiting or parent education, and combination programs that incorporate ECE with home visiting or parent education. The former group includes programs that did not offer early education and generally provide home visiting or parent training in some other setting; the latter group includes programs that offer early childhood education in tandem with home visiting, parent training, or other services. An important difference between the two approaches is that the combination programs generally offered more services—in terms both of the number of contact hours with children and family members and the diversity in the types of treatment.

In terms of the taxonomy of program approaches, our full set of 20 programs includes one program that was exclusively an early education program (Oklahoma Pre-K), so we did not include this program in the analysis. For Project CARE, we included both program models, one in each program approach. Eliminating the four programs without a cognitive measure (see Figure 3.1) gives us 15 programs that measured cognitive outcomes for treated and control children. Six of these were home visiting/parent education programs, and nine were combination programs.

Because the program evaluations followed participants for varying lengths of time, one issue is at what age to measure the outcomes. Given the emphasis of these programs on school readiness and the fact that most evaluations included some measures at the time of school entry, we follow the same selection criteria as in Figure 3.1 and use the first measure available closest to ages 5 or 6. Again, for programs that did not follow children to age 6, we use a measure at approximately age 3. See Appendix B for more details on the methods for this analysis.

As reported in Table 3.7, we find that the combination programs yield better achievement test outcomes on average, but the advantage of the combination programs is not statistically significant at conventional levels. The mean pooled effect size for the combination programs, based on random-effects meta-analysis, was 0.325 compared with a mean pooled effect size of 0.212 for the parent training-only programs—a difference that is not statistically significant. This result is unchanged when we undertake several sensitivity analyses. For instance, the results are not sensitive to excluding from the sample either the CCDP program (because of concerns about the evaluation methodology) or the CPC program (because it is the only quasi-experimental evaluation). Results are also similar when we drop either the Reach Out and Read or DARE to be You programs because their outcome measures (and hence their effect sizes) are least comparable to the other programs. Finally, we find comparable results when we exclude the Houston PCDC program, because it measures outcomes at the oldest age, or when we explicitly control for age in the regression model to account for the possibility of bias resulting from fade-out of cognitive benefits. In all cases, there is a measured advantage

Table 3.7
Mean Achievement Test Effect Size for Combination Programs and Parent Training Programs

Type of Program	Pooled Effect Size	Asymptotic p-Value	Number of Programs
Combination (home visiting/ parent education and ECE)	0.325	0.001	9
Home visiting/parent education only	0.212	0.041	6
Meta-analysis regression coefficient for difference	0.149	0.398	

SOURCE: Authors' calculations using random-effects meta-analysis.
NOTES: Tests of homogeneity of distributions for combination programs rejected at the p = 0.000 level and for parent training only programs rejected at the p = 0.012 level. See Appendix B for more details.

for the combination programs, but the difference is never statistically significant.

Given the small amount of data available for this inquiry, this lack of statistical significance for the difference in the mean effect sizes is not surprising. It is also consistent with the results noted above for the Nelson, Westhues, and MacLeod (2003) meta-analysis. At this point, we can conclude from these results that both program approaches improve outcomes but that there is some indication that combination programs are likely to boost cognitive outcomes more than parenting programs alone. This is not an unexpected result: It is tantamount to saying that when more services are provided, we are more likely to see greater improvement.

Because of the limited data available, we are unable to draw specific conclusions from these results regarding minimum amounts of program intensity or optimal program intensity. However, it is likely a minimum amount of home visits or early childhood education is required to elicit an effect on children's outcomes. At the same time, there is also likely to be a point at which there are diminishing returns to additional service provision. The findings from the Hill, Brooks-Gunn, and Waldfogel (2003) analysis of the IHDP indicate that more intensive services, measured on a low-high dichotomy, produced stronger results. Evaluations of the CPC program, however, have found that attending CPC preschools in the first year provides a big boost to children's outcomes and that participation in the second year still improves outcomes, but not as much as in the first year (Reynolds, 1995, 1997). Similarly, children in the Perry Preschool program who participated for two years realized larger gains than children who participated for one year, but the gains from two years were less than twice the gain from one year of attendance (Berrueta-Clement et al., 1984). These relationships between program intensity and outcomes may not be found in all such intervention programs or for other subgroups of at-risk children. The results do suggest, however, that we need to better understand the relationship between the intensity and duration of program services and program effects for various outcomes.

Both the evidence from the existing literature and our analysis of characteristics that contribute to program effectiveness must be considered preliminary, primarily because we lack enough data to draw firm conclusions. The thin evidence that is available suggests that more is better: Programs with better-trained and more-educated staff and those that provide more services and higher-intensity services produce better outcomes, at least up to a point. However, this does not imply that only the most comprehensive high-intensity programs should be implemented. The question is whether the additional benefits that better programs provide are worth the additional costs or, where resources are constrained, whether some benefits could be achieved by an intervention of modest cost. Although we do not have adequate information to answer such questions, we can address other questions related to the relative costs and benefits of these programs. We turn to these issues in the next chapter.

CHAPTER FOUR

The Economics of Early Childhood Interventions

When considering investing early in the lives of children, particularly those at risk of poor outcomes later in childhood or during the transition to adulthood, it may be enough for some decisionmakers that programs have been demonstrated to generate significant improvements in outcomes in the short term or long term. For them, the evidence presented in Chapter Three provides sufficient justification for devoting significant resources to early childhood intervention programs. Others, however, may believe that constraints on available resources require that programs be justified on economic grounds. For example, will a dollar invested today generate savings down the road to the government or society as a whole that can pay back that initial investment? Are there other economic benefits from early childhood investments that may not easily translate into dollar terms but may be significant nonetheless?

In this chapter, we consider the economic case for investing in early childhood interventions. First, we provide an overview of how early childhood interventions can generate dollar benefits in the near term or longer term—benefits that can be totaled and compared with program costs. Benefit-cost analysis is one approach for comparing the dollar streams of benefits and costs across a range of early investment strategies. Second, we review the evidence from existing benefit-costs studies of early childhood interventions to determine the range of economic returns that have been demonstrated for model programs as well as larger-scale programs. Third, we consider some of the other economic, and even noneconomic, benefits that may accrue from such programs but that typically are not captured in benefit-cost studies. We conclude the chapter by assessing the strengths and limitations of this body of evidence.

Potential Economic Benefits of Early Childhood Interventions

As discussed in Chapter Three, early childhood intervention programs have been demonstrated to produce a range of benefits, in the short term and longer term, both for participating children and, in some cases, for other family members as well. These benefits may accrue in such domains as cognition and academic achievement, behavioral and emotional outcomes, educational progression and attainment, economic success, criminal behavior, health-related behaviors and outcomes, and child maltreatment.

In the remainder of this section, we first focus on the range of spillover benefits that may accrue from the favorable effects of early childhood interventions on the lives of participants. We then discuss the use of benefit-cost analysis as a way of quantifying the total dollar value of these benefits as compared with program costs.

Spillover Benefits and Beneficiaries

Most often, evaluations of early childhood interventions focus on outcomes for participating children. But, as noted in Chapter Three, some of them also assess outcomes for parents. Although most studies do not consider ways other family members benefit, it is plausible that programs may improve outcomes for descendents (e.g., children and grandchildren) of participants (Belfield, 2005). Many of these outcomes affected by early childhood intervention programs can generate spillover benefits (in some cases, costs as well) that can often be quantified in dollar terms. Some of these spillovers may generate public benefits—in other words, savings to the government in the form of reduced outlays for costly programs or services, or additional sources of revenue (e.g., through higher taxes paid). In other cases, the benefits may accrue to private individuals, either the program par-

ticipants themselves or other members of society who did not participate in the program.

Table 4.1 illustrates the range of potential spillover benefits associated with early childhood intervention programs. In particular, it
summarizes key outcomes that may be affected by early childhood
programs and the associated spillover benefit (or cost) that can be
valued in dollar terms. On the left side of the table, a series of columns indicate whose outcome changes—the participating child or
the parent(s) or descendent(s) of the participating child. On the right
side of the table, a series of columns denotes the beneficiaries of the
spillover benefits—the government, program participants, or the rest
of society (i.e., nonparticipants).

For example, when an early childhood intervention program
(such as home visits offering parenting education) leads to a reduction in child maltreatment (second row of Table 4.1), it generates
lower costs for the child welfare system (e.g., foster home care and
case management expenses) and lowers the tangible and intangible
costs to victims of abuse.[1] The savings to the child welfare system
benefit the government (i.e., taxpayers), and program participants
who experience less child abuse receive the gains from lower victim
costs. Improved outcomes for participating children mean that when
they reach adulthood and become parents, they may be less likely to
maltreat their own children. Hence, there is a potential for intergenerational benefits as well (Wolfe and Haveman, 2002).

Table 4.1 shows 13 outcomes that generate such spillover benefits and that are quantifiable in dollar terms. The first outcome, the
value of child care received, is primarily relevant for center-based
early childhood education programs. The time children spend in
these programs is of private value to the parents of the participating
child as a form of child care. The next five outcomes are relevant to
participating children during their childhood and include child

---

[1] Tangible victim costs include those associated with medical care, lost work time, and other
such costs. Intangible victim costs include pain and suffering and other aspects that affect the
victim's quality of life.

Table 4.1
Potential Spillover Benefits and Costs of Improved Outcomes from Early Childhood Intervention Programs

Whose Outcome Changes?			Outcome Affected	Spillover Benefits (Costs)	Beneficiary		
Parent(s) of participant	Participating child	Descendent(s) of participant			Government	Participants	Rest of society
X			Increased child care	Value of subsidized child care for parents of participating children		X	
	X	X	Reduced child maltreatment	Lower costs to child welfare system and lower abuse victim costs	X	X	
	X	X	Reduced child accidents and injuries	Lower costs for emergency room visits and other public health care costs	X	X	
	X	X	Reduced incidence of teen childbearing	Lower costs for public health care system and social welfare programs	X		
	X	X	Reduced grade repetition	Fewer years spent in K–12 education	X		
	X	X	Reduced use of special education	Lower costs for special education	X		
X	X	X	Increased high school graduation rate	(More years spent in K–12 education when dropping out is avoided)	(X)		
X	X	X	Increased college attendance rate	(More years spent in postsecondary education)	(X)	(X)	
X	X	X	Increased labor force participation and earnings in adulthood	Increased lifetime earnings for participants (net of taxes) and increased tax revenue to government	X	X	

Table 4.1—continued

Whose Outcome Changes?			Outcome Affected	Spillover Benefits (Costs)	Beneficiary		
Parent(s) of participant	Participating child	Descendent(s) of participant			Government	Participants	Rest of society
X	X	X	Reduced use of welfare and other means-tested programs	Reduced administrative costs for social welfare programs; reduced welfare program transfer payments	X	(X)	
X	X	X	Reduced crime and contact with criminal justice system	Lower costs for criminal justice systems and lower crime victim costs	X		X
X	X	X	Reduced incidence of smoking and substance abuse	Lower costs for public health care system and from premature death	X	X	
X	X	X	Improved pregnancy outcomes	Lower medical costs due to fewer low-birthweight babies	X		

NOTE: Parentheses denote spillover costs as opposed to benefits.

maltreatment, accidents and injuries, teen childbearing, and school performance (i.e., grade repetition and special education use). Improvements in each of these outcomes benefit the government; the first two also benefit participants. Since these outcomes occur at younger ages, we do not expect most of them to improve for parents of participating children. However, these same outcomes could also improve for future generations.

The remaining seven outcomes all pertain to adulthood. They include educational attendance and attainment (both high school and college), labor force behavior, use of social welfare programs, criminality, smoking and substance abuse, and childbearing. As with the previous outcomes in childhood, early childhood interventions may generate improvements in these outcomes for both participating children and their descendents. However, parents may also demonstrate improvements in these outcomes as a result of an early childhood program. They too may obtain more human capital; experience improved labor market, health, and pregnancy outcomes; and impose lower costs on society from crime and welfare use.

Two of these outcomes—improvements in high school graduation and college attendance rates—differ from the others in that they are associated with spillover costs.[2] Whether the parents of participating children or the children themselves obtain a high school diploma or attend college, the additional educational attainment results in added public education costs, as well as private education costs (e.g., for college tuition). These costs are offset by the gains to the individuals from higher earnings associated with more human capital (net of taxes paid) and to the public sector from the higher taxes paid on the increased earnings (shown elsewhere in the table).

Reductions in welfare use and the use of other means-tested programs produce offsetting benefits and costs. Taxpayers gain from the reduced outlays for such programs and the savings in administra-

---

[2] These two outcomes may also lead to indirect spillover benefits such as higher employment rates, earnings, and so on. These outcomes, related to improved educational attainment, are shown elsewhere in the table. So the direct effect is the costs associated with attaining the higher levels of schooling.

tive costs. However, program participants, who rely less on these programs as a result of an early childhood intervention, no longer have that source of income or in-kind benefit. Thus, the reduction in the pure transfer payment (or in-kind benefit) is a benefit for taxpayers but an equal and offsetting cost for participants. Since taxpayers also gain from the reduction in administrative costs, there is an overall benefit in the form of administrative cost savings, when viewed from the perspective of society as a whole. This will generally be smaller than the transfer payment itself.[3]

The primary way that nonparticipants benefit from early childhood interventions—ways that can be quantified in dollar terms at least—is through reduction in crime. For the potential crime victims ("rest of society" column), the crimes averted generate both tangible benefits (e.g., less property loss, lost work time, and medical care) and intangible benefits (e.g., less pain and suffering).

It is worth noting that the range of outcomes enumerated in Table 4.1 that may generate monetary benefits to taxpayers, participants, or the rest of the society is more limited than many of the outcomes typically measured in evaluations of early childhood intervention programs (see the discussion in Chapter Three). Although early childhood interventions may generate improvements in children's cognitive functioning or behavior and other socioemotional outcomes, these improvements do not readily translate into dollar gains for the stakeholders listed in Table 4.1. Moreover, almost all the outcomes in Table 4.1 that pertain to participating children are not seen until the children grow older, including many that are not observed until they reach adulthood. (This is less so for the parental outcomes, which may improve even when the children are very young.) Conse-

---

[3] A similar point can be made about taxes, but in reverse. Any increase in tax payments to government is simply a transfer away from individuals. Thus, any earnings gains for participants should be measured net of taxes paid. Economists point out that taxes may also generate deadweight losses (comparable to the administrative costs of transfer payments). The deadweight losses arise from the costs of collecting taxes and the distortionary effects of taxes on behavior (e.g., higher taxes are expected to reduce work effort). The administrative costs of tax collection are typically not accounted for in benefit-cost studies of early childhood programs. Any distortionary effects should be captured in the estimates of program effects (e.g., on earnings).

quently, efforts to assess the full range of spillover benefits in Table 4.1 require either long-term follow-up of participants in early childhood programs or the ability to make predictions about improvements in these longer-term outcomes based on improvements in outcomes at younger ages.

The Use of Benefit-Cost Analysis

The range of potential spillover benefits (and in some cases costs) associated with early childhood interventions that can be expressed in monetary terms suggests that it is possible to compare the total costs of implementing an early childhood program with total benefits. Benefit-cost analysis is designed to allow such comparisons. In particular, it is a tool that can be used to compare, for a given stakeholder, the total value of the benefits of a particular policy, relative to a given baseline, with the costs of the policy, again relative to the baseline. Dollars provide a common unit of measurement for tallying all costs and benefits, and all values are adjusted for inflation. The dollar benefits of a program associated with a given outcome are derived from the effect of the program on that outcome (as assessed, for example, in a randomized experiment where program effects are measured relative to a control group, the baseline) and the dollar value associated with a change in the outcome.

Given that program costs and benefits can occur at different points in time (e.g., upfront costs with benefits that accrue into the future), all dollar figures are discounted at a constant annual rate to a common point in time (e.g., the age of the child at the start of the program). This discounting converts all dollar figures into present-value terms. In other words, since receiving a dollar in the future is not as attractive as receiving a dollar today, future dollars are worth less than today's dollars. The farther into the future a dollar is received, the less it is worth in today's dollars. Discount rates of 3 to 6 percent per year are typically used in benefit-cost analyses of social policy programs (Karoly et al., 2001), where higher discount rates imply that future dollars are worth even less than would be the case with a lower discount rate.

In addition to comparing the total present value of benefits and costs, other summary measures from benefit-cost studies include net benefits (the difference between present-value benefits and present-value costs, also known as net present value), and the benefit-cost ratio.[4] A benefit-cost ratio that exceeds 1 is equivalent to net benefits being greater than zero.

A simple example can be used to illustrate how the benefit-cost calculation is made. Consider an early childhood intervention program with a rigorous evaluation (e.g., a randomized experiment) showing that participation in the program for one year at age 4 reduces years of special education used between ages 6 and 15 by 0.5 years on average (i.e., special education usage is lower by half a year for the treatment group compared with the control group). If a year of special education in 2003 dollars costs $10,000 more per child than a year in a regular classroom, the half-year reduction in special education use produces a savings of $5,000 per child served. The $5,000 savings needs to be applied at the specific age or ages that the savings occurs. In this example, we use the midpoint of the age interval over which the effect is measured (in this case age 10). The value of $5,000 accrued at age 10 would be discounted at a fixed rate (say 3 percent per year) from age 10 to age 4 of the child, so it can be compared with the upfront program costs incurred at age 4. In this case, the present value of the savings in special education costs is $4,065 per child in 2003 dollars, discounting to age 4 using a 3-percent discount rate. If the cost of the one-year program is $2,000, then the program generates net benefits of $2,065 per child and a benefit-cost ratio of 2.03, or a return of $2.03 for every dollar invested. In this example, just one source of spillover benefits is included (i.e., special education use). Other benefit (or cost) streams can be included as well, each based on the estimated program effect, the estimated dollar benefit (or costs) associated with that effect, and

---

[4] Another summary measure that is sometimes calculated is the internal rate of return (IRR) (see, for example, Rolnick and Grunewald, 2003). The IRR is the discount rate at which the net present value (present-value benefits minus present-value costs) equals zero. The IRR will exceed the discount rate when net benefits are greater than zero.

the associated discounting, depending on the time path over which the dollar benefits (or costs) accrue.

The comparison of benefits and costs, and the summary measures, can be calculated for society as a whole or for different stakeholders, such as the government (e.g., public sector) or the private sector (e.g., program participants and nonparticipants). As noted in Table 4.1, some of the effects of early childhood programs may generate little benefit to society overall because there are offsetting benefits to different segments of society, such as the government and participants (welfare benefits were the example noted earlier). Thus, the distribution of benefits and costs across stakeholders may be of interest.

In the context of early childhood intervention programs, benefit-cost analyses are limited by the range of benefits that can be monetized (Karoly et al., 2001). Although costs may be easy to measure, the benefits—especially those that accrue far in the future—may not be readily available, especially if there has been no long-term follow-up. If early childhood programs are evaluated when the participants are still young and long-term outcomes have not been observed and cannot be reasonably predicted, measures of their present-value benefits are often incomplete and hence very low. Even when there is long-term follow-up, evaluations may focus on outcomes for participating children, with less information about potential benefits to parents or descendents. In addition, the monetary value of some benefits can be controversial. For example, reductions in crime are associated with tangible benefits to potential crime victims (e.g., reduction in injury, lost work time), but there may be intangible benefits as well (e.g., reduction in pain and suffering). The latter type of benefit is harder to value and therefore is sometimes omitted from benefit-cost studies (Karoly et al., 1998).

Benefit-cost analysis has other limitations more generally that should be kept in mind as well. While the analysis may look at benefits and costs from the standpoint of different stakeholders, the approach generally places equal weight on benefits, regardless of who gains. Thus, distributional concerns of decisionmakers are generally not accounted for. Indeed, benefit-cost analysis is typically conducted from the perspective of a hypothetical "social planner," where the weights attached to the benefits and costs that accrue to different stakeholders are assumed to be those of this benevolent decision-maker.

The notion of a social planner also abstracts from the real-world problems that arise when the costs of an early childhood program are borne by one stakeholder and the benefits accrue to another. For example, program costs may be covered by the public sector, whereas the benefits are realized by private individuals, either participants or nonparticipants. In other cases, all the benefits and costs may accrue within the public sector but are distributed across different public agencies. Program costs may come out of the health and human services department's budgets, but the downstream savings are realized by the education and public safety departments. This misalignment in costs and benefits across the various stovepipes of the public sector, or between the public and private sectors, makes it difficult to find the support among all the needed parties for investing in an early childhood intervention.

Benefit-cost analysis also typically does not consider the possible role of altruism in the valuation of program benefits. Some members of society may value the benefits of an early childhood program that accrue to participants even if they do not directly experience any personal gain (e.g., through reduced crime rates). Such valuations are difficult to measure, and there is little empirical basis for making estimates in the early childhood field. Evidence from other areas of social policy suggest that altruistic valuations may be at least as large as the private valuations typically accounted for (Viscusi, Magat, and Forrest, 1988).

Benefit-Cost Studies of Early Childhood Interventions

Benefit-cost analyses have been conducted for a subset of the 20 programs discussed in earlier chapters.[5] In this section, we review the re-

---

[5] Benefit-cost analyses have also been conducted for potential early childhood programs, such as a universal preschool program in California (Karoly and Bigelow, 2005), New York

sults from those analyses to determine the extent to which early childhood intervention programs can be justified on economic grounds. Before presenting results for these studies, standardized to make them as comparable as possible, we first highlight some methodological differences that can affect the ability to make valid comparisons across studies.

Programs Analyzed and Methods Used

Table 4.2 summarizes the early childhood interventions that have associated benefit-cost studies, noting the age at last follow-up of the participants, the age to which benefits and costs are discounted, the discount rate, and the year in which dollar values are denominated. Among the programs that provide home visiting or parent education, Aos et al. (2004) conduct a benefit-cost analysis for the HIPPY USA program and for the full sample of the NFP program, and Karoly et al. (1998) present results for higher-risk and lower-risk samples participating in the NFP program.[6] Aos et al. (2004) also include benefit-cost estimates for home visiting programs for at-risk mothers and children more generally, based on a meta-analysis of 13 such programs. Among programs that combine home visiting or parent education with ECE, benefit-cost analyses have been conducted for the CCDP and IHDP by Aos et al. (2004), the Carolina Abecedarian program by Masse and Barnett (2002), and the Chicago CPC by Reynolds et al. (2002). Benefit-cost studies of the Perry Preschool program include analyses based on the age-27 follow-up data by Karoly et al. (1998), Barnett (1993), and Schweinhart, Barnes, and Weikart (1993) and based on the age-40 follow-up data by Barnett, Belfield, and Nores (2005). Aos et al. (2004) also include a meta-analysis of 48 early childhood education programs for three- and

---

(Belfield, 2004a), and Ohio (Belfield, 2004b). These analyses typically draw on the program effects from one or more of the programs reviewed in Chapter 3.

[6] The Karoly et al. (1998) benefit-cost analysis was based on the Elmira trial of the NFP, referenced as the Elmira PEIP. The evaluation of the Elmira PEIP provided separate results for a sample of higher-risk first-time mothers (those who were unmarried and had low SES) and a lower-risk sample (all other sample members, generally those who were either single or had low SES).

Table 4.2
Benefit-Cost Analyses of Early Childhood Intervention Programs

Early Childhood Program	Study Citation	Age at Last Follow-Up	Discount to Age...	Discount Rate (%)	Dollar Year
Home Visiting/Parent Education					
HIPPY USA	Aos et al. (2004)	6	3	3	2003
NFP	Karoly et al. (1998)	15	0	4, 0–8	1996
NFP	Aos et al. (2004)	15	0	3	2003
Home visiting for at-risk mothers and children (meta-analysis of 13 programs)	Aos et al. (2004)	Varies (age 15 max.)	0	3	2003
Home Visiting/Parent Education Combined with ECE					
CCDP	Aos et al. (2004)	5	0	3	2003
IHDP	Aos et al. (2004)	8	0	3	2003
Abecedarian	Masse and Barnett (2002)	21	0	3, 5, 7	2002
Chicago CPC	Reynolds et al. (2002)	21	3	3	1998
Perry Preschool	Karoly et al. (1998)	27	0	4, 0–8	1996
Perry Preschool	Barnett (1993); Schweinhart, Barnes, and Weikart (1993)	27	3	3	1992
Perry Preschool	Barnett, Belfield, and Nores (2005)	40	3	0, 3, 7	2000
Early childhood education (ECE) for low-income three- and four-year-olds (meta-analysis of 48 programs)	Aos et al. (2004)	Varies (age 27 max.)	3	3	2003

SOURCE: Authors' tabulations based on sources cited in table and Appendix A.
NOTES: See Table 2.2 for full program names.

four-year olds, from which they generate a benefit-cost estimate for this generic program model.

When comparing outcomes from these analyses (ten studies for seven specific programs and two for generic program types), it is important to keep in mind key differences in the information available for each program and methods used, differences that may affect estimates of net program benefits and benefit-cost ratios. First, there are the underlying differences in the evaluation methodologies discussed in Chapters Two and Three. For example, of the specific programs listed in Table 4.2, the CPC evaluation uses a quasi-experimental design, and problems with the execution of the experimental design for the CCDP program have been identified. The estimates of outcome effects for the meta-analysis of home visiting programs and of early childhood education programs by Aos et al. (2004) are based on program evaluations of varying quality. Another evaluation difference is the variation in baseline services offered. As noted in Chapter Two, Abecedarian, Project CARE, and IHDP provided some health, developmental, or family services to the control group, so the program costs and benefits are relative to a baseline that includes some remedial services. This would tend to lower the program effects and therefore the dollar benefits compared with a baseline in other program evaluations where such services are not offered.[7]

Second, Table 4.2 shows that the follow-up periods available for the benefit-cost analyses range from as short as to age 5 in the CCDP analysis to as long as to age 27 or 40 in the Perry Preschool study. Longer follow-ups are also available for the NFP (age 15), Abecedarian (age 21), and Chicago CPC (age 21). Those studies with longer-term follow-up are more likely to be able to measure many of the outcomes included in Table 4.1 that generate economic benefits to various stakeholders. Studies with only short-term follow-up may include only outcomes that cannot be readily translated into dollar val-

---

[7] Because program costs should be measured relative to the baseline, they should also be lower compared with an intervention that includes the baseline services for the treatment group only. The effect on net benefits will depend on the value of the marginal benefit of the baseline services versus the costs of those services.

ues. Therefore, net benefits and benefit-cost ratios are likely to be lower for studies with shorter follow-up periods.

Third, the studies use different methods for discounting dollars in terms of the reference age, discount rate, and year for which dollars are valued. Studies typically discount benefits and costs to the year children begin participating in a program. Thus, as seen in Table 4.2, those programs that start at birth—most of the home visiting/parent education programs and the CCDP, IHDP, and Abecedarian programs—discount to age 0. With the exception of the Karoly et al. (1998) study of the Perry Preschool program, the other studies in Table 4.2—all ECE programs that start a year or two before kindergarten entry—discount to age 3. In terms of discount rates, most studies report results for one rate, typically 3 or 4 percent; a few present estimates for discount rates that range between 0 and 8 percent. Finally, results are reported in 1992 dollars up to 2003 dollars. In the comparison of results that we present below, we adjust for these methodological differences across studies by discounting all benefits and costs to age 0 using a 3 percent discount rate with all dollar values converted to 2003 dollars.[8]

Fourth, while all studies have access to comprehensive measures of program costs, the studies vary in the benefits that are valued and the extent to which benefits are based on observed outcomes and/or projected beyond the follow-up period. Table 4.3 summarizes the spillover benefits (and costs, in some cases) that are measured in the 12 studies. The categories in the table mirror those included in Table 4.1, with the exception of reduced teen childbearing and improved pregnancy outcomes, neither of which was valued in dollar terms in any of the studies (primarily because they were not measured in the program evaluations). For each outcome included in Table 4.3, the cell entries indicate whether the study valued benefits based on

---

[8] The Karoly et al. (1998) study is the only one that does not report results for a 3-percent discount rate, although results were presented for discount rates range from 0 to 8 percent (see Figures 3.7 and 3.8 in that study). To convert all dollars to 2003 values, we use the Consumer Price Index for All Urban Consumers (CPI-U) (see U.S. Department of Labor, undated).

Table 4.3
Benefits (Costs) Included in Selected Benefit-Cost Studies of Early Childhood Intervention Programs

	Home Visiting/Parent Education						Home Visiting/Parent Education Combined with ECE				
Benefits (costs)	HIPPY USA (age 6)	NFP[a] (age 15)	NFP[b] (age 15)	HV (meta) (varies)	CCDP (age 5)	IHDP (age 8)	Abece-darian (age 21)	Chicago CPC (age 21)	Perry Preschool[c] (age 27)	Perry Preschool[d] (age 27/40)	ECE (meta) (varies)
Child care											
Value of child care								C	C	C	C
Child maltreatment											
Child welfare system savings			C*	C*				C			C*
Savings to victims of child maltreatment			C*	C*				C			C*
Child accidents and injuries											
Emergency room visits savings		C									
Other public health care savings											

Table 4.3—continued

Benefits (costs)	Home Visiting/Parent Education						Home Visiting/Parent Education Combined with ECE				
	HIPPY USA (age 6)	NFP[a] (age 15)	NFP[b] (age 15)	HV (meta) (varies)	CCDP (age 5)	IHDP (age 8)	Abece-darian (age 21)	Chicago CPC (age 21)	Perry Preschool[c] (age 27)	Perry Preschool[d] (age 27/40)	ECE (meta) (varies)
Education											
K–12 education savings							C	C	C	C	C
Special education savings							C	C	C	C	C
(Post-secondary education costs)							C	C*	C*	C*	
Employment											
After-tax earnings	C**	P	P*	P*			C**, P*, D**	C**	C*	C*	C*
Taxes on earnings	C**	P	P*	P*			C**, P*, D**	C**	C*	C*	C*

Table 4.3—continued

Benefits (costs)	Home Visiting/Parent Education				Home Visiting/Parent Education Combined with ECE						
	HIPPY USA (age 6)	NFP[a] (age 15)	NFP[b] (age 15)	HV (meta) (varies)	CCDP (age 5)	IHDP (age 8)	Abece-darian (age 21)	Chicago CPC (age 21)	Perry Preschool[c] (age 27)	Perry Preschool[d] (age 27/40)	ECE (meta) (varies)
Social welfare use											
Welfare program administrative costs and transfer payments savings		P			P		C*		C*	C*	
Crime and delinquency											
Justice system savings	C*, P	C*, P*	P*					C*	C*	C*	C*
Tangible savings to victims of crime	C*, P	C*, P*	P*					C*	C*	C*	C*
Intangible savings to victims of crime		C*, P*								C*	

Table 4.3—continued

	Home Visiting/Parent Education				Home Visiting/Parent Education Combined with ECE						
Benefits (costs)	HIPPY USA (age 6)	NFP[a] (age 15)	NFP[b] (age 15)	HV (meta) (varies)	CCDP (age 5)	IHDP (age 8)	Abecedarian (age 21)	Chicago CPC (age 21)	Perry Preschool[c] (age 27)	Perry Preschool[d] (age 27/40)	ECE (meta) (varies)
Smoking and substance abuse											
Public health care savings				P			C				
Savings of private costs of premature death				P			C				

SOURCE: Authors' tabulations based on sources cited in Table 4.2.

NOTES: See Table 2.2 for full program names. Cell symbols indicate the benefit (cost) for this outcome is monetized for the participating child (C), and/or the participating child's parent(s) (P) and/or descendents (D). In the Abecedarian program, descendents are projected for generations two through four.

* Benefit (cost) based both on observed outcomes as of the age of last follow-up and a projection beyond the age the individual was last observed.

** Benefit (cost) based only on a projection beyond the age the individual was last observed.

[a] Karoly et al. (1998).
[b] Aos et al. (2004).
[c] Karoly et al. (1998).
[d] Barnett (1993), Schweinhart, Barnes, and Weikart (1993); Barnett, Belfield, and Nores (2005).

changes in the outcome for the participating child (C), and/or the child's parents (P) or descendents (D). A single asterisk indicates that benefits were based on both observed outcomes and projections beyond the age at last follow-up; a double asterisk, that only projected benefits were measured. (No asterisk means the benefits were based on observed outcomes only.) For example, earnings may be observed up to a certain age and then projected beyond the last age observed, based on observed or expected education levels and other individual characteristics.

As illustrated in the table, most benefits are valued based on changes in outcomes for participating children, and the range of benefits measured is more comprehensive for studies with longer-term follow-up. For example, benefits in adulthood, such as employment outcomes and social welfare program use, are limited to studies with follow-up to early or middle adulthood. Fewer studies value benefits for parents, typically because parental outcomes are not measured. Only the Abecedarian benefit-cost study includes a projection of benefits for descendents of participating children, based on estimates from studies of the intergenerational transmission of earnings. Benefits projected beyond the age at last follow-up are most commonly the earnings of the participating child or the child's parents and the savings to the criminal justice system and victims of crime and, less commonly, to the child welfare system and victims of child maltreatment.[9] When victim costs are considered, several studies are conservative in measuring only the value of averting the tangi-

---

[9] When such projections are made, they are generally calculated with conservative assumptions, and sensitivity analyses are done to see whether results change substantially when alternative assumptions are used. Moreover, since the projected benefits are so far in the future, they are heavily discounted and therefore not a very large part of the estimated total benefits. For example, the results for the Perry Preschool program based on the age-40 follow-up data demonstrate that the actual benefits realized between ages 27 and 40 were much larger than researchers had projected based on the observed outcomes through age 27 (see Barnett, 1993; Schweinhart, Barnes, and Weikart, 1993; and Barnett, Belfield, and Nores, 2005).

ble victim costs, although others include intangible victim costs as well.[10]

Fifth, other aspects of the benefit-cost methodologies vary across the studies as well. Notably, the programs analyzed by Aos et al. (2004) were assessed in the context of benefits for Washington state policymakers. Hence, estimates of benefits were typically based on savings to government and other benefits based on dollar figures for the state of Washington. Likewise, many of the savings estimates for the Chicago CPC program by Reynolds et al. (2002) used cost data relevant for Illinois. In addition, in the Aos et al. (2004) methodology, the program effects reported for each study, converted to effect sizes, are adjusted to account for the quality of the evaluation design and whether the program effects are measured in real-world settings (i.e., effect sizes are scaled back for weaker study designs and small-scale model programs that are conducted in highly controlled research settings). For some programs, the estimated program effects are adjusted to equal zero given the weak evaluation design or the possibility that results might be weaker when the program is implemented on a larger scale. Effect sizes based on meta-analyses of multiple programs also use these adjusted effect sizes. Thus, the estimated benefits based on these effects are arguably more conservative than those estimated in the other studies shown in Table 4.2.

These methodological differences are particularly relevant for three of the programs studied. The benefit-cost analysis of the IHDP conducted by Aos et al. (2004) does not estimate values for any of the benefits shown in Table 4.3. In that case, the only outcome that could potentially generate dollar savings, given the short follow-up period (to age 8), is test scores, and the adjusted effect size is zero. The benefit-cost analyses, also by Aos et al. (2004), of the two other studies with short-term follow-up—CCDP and HIPPY (to ages 5 and 6, respectively)—include just one category of benefits each. The

---

[10] Estimates of the intangible benefits of crime reduction can be much larger than the tangible benefits (for estimates, see Miller, Cohen and Wiersema, 1996).

CCDP includes only the value of a change in welfare use among parents; the estimated effect indicates that welfare usage increased, thereby raising the cost to government. Because the effect for the sole outcome of this program involves higher costs for society as a whole (as a result of the administrative costs of greater welfare payments), the program cannot possibly break even. In the case of the HIPPY USA program, the benefit-cost analysis estimates values for the projected lifetime earnings gain based on the program's effect on test scores at an early age.[11] Barring a large change in the single outcome considered, coupled with considerable savings from the change, this program would be expected to have smaller estimated benefits than the other studies in Table 4.2, which measure multiple sources of benefits.

Results of Benefit-Cost Analyses

Given these differences in methodology, we must be cautious in comparing the results of benefit-cost analyses for the programs cited in Table 4.2. The studies measure considerably different sets of outcomes and therefore do not evaluate a consistent set of benefits, most often due to data limitations. Other methodological differences limit the comparability of the findings as well. So the results should not be used to determine which program or type of program is likely to generate the "biggest bang for the buck." With longer-term follow-up and more-comprehensive assessments of outcomes affected, programs that have low benefit-cost ratios based on information available today could have more favorable results with a more complete accounting. The results can be used, however, to demonstrate whether, in principle, early childhood intervention programs can generate benefits that outweigh the program costs.

Table 4.4 presents the results of the benefit-cost analyses for seven individual programs and two generic program types. The table

---

[11] The CCDP evaluation also measured children's test scores and the HIPPY study measured the effect of the program on special education use. In both cases, however, the adjusted effect sizes calculated by Aos et al. (2004) for these outcomes were zero, so they made no contribution to the value of program benefits.

Table 4.4
Benefit-Cost Results of Selected Early Childhood Intervention Programs

Program	Type	Age at Last Follow-Up	Program Costs per Child ($)	Distribution of Benefits per Child ($)				Total Benefits to Society per Child ($)	Net Benefits to Society per Child ($)	Benefit-Cost Ratio
				Participants	Savings to Government	Rest of Society				
Follow-Up During Elementary School Years										
CCDP	Combo	5	37,388	91	-101	0	-9	-37,397	—
HIPPY USA	HV/PE	6	1,681	1,940	485	607	3,032	1,351	1.80
IHDP	Combo	8	49,021	0	0	0	0	-49,021	—
Follow-Up During Secondary School Years										
NFP—higher-risk sample	HV/PE	15	7,271	1,277	32,447	7,695	41,419	34,148	5.70
NFP—lower-risk sample	HV/PE	15	7,271	2,051	5,095	2,005	9,151	1,880	1.26
NFP—full sample	HV/PE	15	9,118	2,674	9,548	14,075	26,298	17,180	2.88
HV for at-risk mothers and children (meta-analysis)	HV/PE	Varies	4,892	6,194	1,815	2,960	10,969	6,077	2.24

Table 4.4—continued

Program	Type	Age at Last Follow-Up	Program Costs per Child ($)	Distribution of Benefits per Child ($)			Total Benefits to Society per Child ($)	Net Benefits to Society per Child ($)	Benefit-Cost Ratio
				Participants	Savings to Government	Rest of Society			
				Follow-Up to Early Adulthood					
Abecedarian	Combo	21	42,871	n.a.	n.a.	n.a.	138,635	95,764	3.23
Chicago CPC	Combo	21	6,913	22,715	19,985	6,637	49,337	42,424	7.14
Perry Preschool (excluding intangible crime costs)	Combo	27	14,830	22,599	37,724	16,104	76,426	61,595	5.15
Perry Preschool (including intangible crime costs)	Combo	27	14,830	23,486	106,136		129,622	114,792	8.74
ECE for low-income three- and four-year-olds (meta-analysis)	Combo	Varies	6,681	6,036	4,329	5,377	15,742	9,061	2.36

Table 4.4—continued

	Type	Age at Last Follow-Up	Program Costs per Child ($)	Distribution of Benefits per Child ($)			Total Benefits to Society per Child ($)	Net Benefits to Society per Child ($)	Benefit-Cost Ratio
Program				Participants	Savings to Government	Rest of Society			
Follow-Up to Middle Adulthood									
Perry Preschool	Combo	40	14,830	61,866	191,288		253,154	238,324	17.07

SOURCE: Author's calculations based on Karoly et al. (1998), Table 3.7 (NFP high- and low-risk and Perry Preschool excluding intangible crime costs); Masse and Barnett (2002), Table 8.2 (Abecedarian); Reynolds et al. (2002), Table 5 (Chicago CPC); Barnett (1993), Table 3 (Perry Preschool age 21 follow-up including intangible crime costs); Barnett, Belfield, and Nores (2005), Table 7.8 (Perry Preschool age 40 follow-up); and Aos et al. (2004), Table 1 and Appendix (all other programs).

NOTES: See Table 2.2 for full program names. All dollar values are 2003 dollars per child and are the present value of amounts over time where future values are discounted to age 0 of the participating child, using a 3 percent annual real discount rate. Numbers may not sum due to rounding. n.a. = not available; Combo = HV/parent education combined with ECE; ECE = early childhood education; HV = home visiting; PE = parent education.

first records the program type according to our taxonomy and the age at last follow-up. The remaining columns show the estimated present value of the costs of each program (or type of program) per child and the present value of total program benefits per child for society as a whole, all in 2003 dollars discounted to age 0 using a 3 percent real discount rate. The distribution of total benefits to society is also shown, accounting for the amount of present-value benefits per child that accrue to participants, to government, and to the rest of society (i.e., nonparticipants). Net benefits per child are shown as well (based on the total benefits to society), along with the benefit-cost ratio. In recognition of the differing follow-up periods, the results are presented in four panels based on the age of participants at the time of the last follow-up: the elementary school years, the secondary school years, early adulthood, and middle adulthood.[12]

As seen in the third column of the table, the programs vary considerably in terms of present-value cost, from less than $2,000 per child for the HIPPY program to nearly $50,000 per child for the IHDP. These cost differences reflect, in part, the differential intensity of resources used based on the length of time over which services were delivered (e.g., up to five years from birth to school entry or for shorter periods of time) and the hours of services delivered during those ages. Likewise, measured present value total benefits to society also vary across programs, from –$9 and $0 per child, respectively, for the CCDP and IHDP (noted above for the shorter follow-up periods, limited outcomes measured, and lack of favorable effects in the case of CCDP) to over $250,000 per child for the Perry Preschool program based on the age-40 results (the program with the longest follow-up period). Consequently, net benefits range from negative numbers (for CCDP and IHDP) to large positive numbers (notably for Perry Preschool). Eliminating the two programs for which the benefit-cost ratio is not applicable (because of zero or negative benefits), the ratio ranges from 1.80 for HIPPY to 17.07 for Perry Preschool.

---

[12] For the results based on the meta-analysis, the age at last follow-up varies, so we rely on the oldest age among the studies included.

The distribution of present-value benefits between different stakeholders is available for all but the Abecedarian program. (In the case of the Perry Preschool results at age 27—when intangible crime costs are included—and at age 40, the savings to government are combined with benefits to the rest of society.) Excluding CCDP and IHDP, all programs generate positive benefits to participants, government, and the rest of society. Where they are disaggregated, the benefits to participants are substantial in the case of Perry Preschool (regardless of the study) and Chicago CPC (from about $23,000 to $62,000 per child). The savings to government, while positive (aside from the two exceptions), are not always large enough to cover the costs of the program. This is the case for the NFP lower-risk sample, the HIPPY USA program, and the generic home visit and ECE programs based on the Aos et al. (2004) meta-analysis. In these cases, although total benefits to society exceed the program costs, the measured savings to government would not be enough to pay for the cost of the program.

It is important to emphasize again the underlying differences in methodology used to generate the results in Table 4.4. Notably, programs with longer follow-up periods tend to have higher estimates of total benefits, net benefits, and benefit-cost ratio. As noted earlier, programs such as Abecedarian, Chicago CPC, and Perry Preschool can measure outcomes at older ages that are more readily translated into dollar benefits, with possibly substantial savings to all stakeholders. These include such favorable outcomes as higher earnings through early adulthood or middle adulthood (a benefit to participants and taxpayers resulting from higher tax payments), reduced reliance on social welfare programs (a benefit to taxpayers), and reduced contact with the criminal justice system (a benefit to both taxpayers and other members of society). A comparison of the results for the Perry Preschool program at ages 27 and 40 clearly illustrates the benefit of long-term follow-up. With longer follow-up, the net benefits and benefit-cost ratio for Perry Preschool more than double: from $115,000 to $238,000 in net benefits per participant and from $8.74 to $17.07 in benefits for every dollar invested. This is because the actual earnings gains and reduced criminal activity measured between ages 27 and 40 were even larger than researchers had predicted, based on outcomes observed at age 27. The choice of which benefits to value can also make a difference. Based on the age-27 follow-up, the estimated benefit-cost ratio for the Perry Preschool program ranges from 5.15 to 8.74, where the intangible crime savings are excluded from the former figure but included in the latter.

Despite these differences in methodology and the resulting variation in the estimated net benefits and benefit-cost ratios, the results demonstrate several key findings with respect to the economics of early childhood investments. First, it is possible in principle for early childhood interventions to generate short-term and longer-terms benefits that can more than offset program costs. Two of the three individual home visiting/parent education programs analyzed have generated positive net benefits. When results are combined across multiple evaluations of home visiting programs and even when conservative assumptions about average program effects are used, as in the Aos et al. (2004) meta-analysis, home visiting programs are estimated to generate about $6,000 in net benefits per child, or $2.24 for every dollar invested. Likewise, three of the four specific programs that combined home visiting/parent education and ECE were shown to generate positive net benefits. Again, the Aos et al. (2004) meta-analysis of early childhood education programs for disadvantaged three- and four-year olds conservatively estimates a return of nearly $16,000 in net benefits per child, or $2.36 for every dollar invested. Those programs without favorable net benefits or benefit-cost ratios are either ineffective (e.g., CCDP) or limited in the outcomes available to express in monetary terms (e.g., IHDP).

Second, the favorable economic returns from early childhood intervention programs are not limited to smaller-scale demonstration programs. It is true that the largest estimated return is for the relatively small-scale Perry Preschool program as of the age-40 follow-up (nearly $240,000 in net benefits per child, or a return of just over $17 for every dollar invested). This program has the longest follow-up period, and the benefit-cost ratio increases as it moves from estimates based on follow-up data through age 27 to data based on the age-40 follow-up. However, the larger-scale Chicago CPC program is estimated to generate over $42,000 in net benefits per child, or $7.14 for every dollar invested. The CPC, implemented in the Chicago public school system, demonstrates that economic benefits can accrue for programs that operate in multiple sites under public auspices.

Third, favorable benefit-cost ratios are achieved for both higher-cost, more-intensive programs and lower-cost, less-intensive programs. The Abecedarian program is one of the most intensive programs among those with benefit-cost analyses, with full-time year-round center-based care provided from soon after birth up through kindergarten entry. Despite the high cost of that intensive set of services, the program generates benefits to society that are over three times its costs—equal to nearly $96,000 in net benefits per child. In contrast, the HIPPY program is the lowest-cost intervention with a benefit-cost analysis, yet it too is estimated to generate benefits to society of nearly $2 for every dollar invested, although net benefits per child are just about $1,400.

Fourth, there is some evidence in Table 4.4 that effectively targeting program services generates more-favorable economic outcomes. The benefit-cost analysis of the NFP program conducted by Karoly et al. (1998) estimated results separately for both a higher-risk sample of mothers and children served and a lower-risk sample. Because the categories of benefits estimated for those two subsamples were the same, a comparison of the benefit-cost results can be made without concern for differences in methodology. As seen in Table 4.4, the net benefits per child were about 18 times as great for the higher-risk sample ($34,148 versus $1,880), and the benefit-cost ratios were 5.70 and 1.26 for the higher-risk and lower-risk samples, respectively. These differences in results are due solely to the differential effect of the early childhood program on the higher-risk versus the lower-risk populations.

Other evidence of the relevance of targeting comes from studies that project the economic returns from universal programs. For example, the analyses by Karoly and Bigelow (2005) and Belfield (2004b) suggest that the returns from a universal preschool program would be less than those measured for programs that serve a more-disadvantaged population. Nonetheless, the net benefits for society as a whole in both universal preschool studies are still estimated to be positive, and the corresponding benefit-cost ratios exceed 1.

Finally, we note that the discussion in Chapter Three of the potential for declining returns associated with increased program intensity is also relevant for benefit-cost calculations. For example, the benefit-cost ratio of 7.14 for the Chicago CPC program presented in Table 4.4 is based on a sample of children who, on average, had attended 1.5 years of preschool. Estimates provided by Reynolds et al. (2002) indicate that the benefit-cost ratio for the CPC program participants who attended for just one year was 12.02, compared with 5.02 when children were in the program for two years.

Other Economic and Noneconomic Benefits of Early Childhood Interventions

Benefit-cost analysis can be extremely useful in demonstrating the economic returns from investing in early childhood interventions. As noted in the previous section, such estimates may be conservative because data limitations often preclude measuring the economic benefits associated with all the potential benefits from changes in outcomes for participants, their parents, and their descendents. Benefit-cost analyses typically do not account for other economic and noneconomic benefits of early childhood interventions. In this section, we focus on potential labor market and macroeconomic benefits, as well as broader social benefits.

Labor Market Benefits

Early childhood programs that provide full-time care for children prior to kindergarten entry have the potential to increase the size of the workforce and improve labor market performance for workers with young children—benefits to the parents of children who participate in early childhood programs as well as to their employers (see Karoly and Bigelow, 2005, for a recent review of the literature). Full-day preschool programs and the Abecedarian program, which provided full-time care soon after birth until kindergarten entry, are both relevant examples. Research indicates that women's labor force participation rates increase as child care costs decline—more so for single mothers and for low-wage women (see Blau, 2001, and Anderson and Levine, 2000, for reviews). The stability and quality of child care options can also affect the decision to work or not, as well as performance on the job. For example, a limited research base suggests that job turnover and absenteeism may improve for workers who have access to more formal, dependable sources of child care (Karoly and Bigelow, 2005).

The research evidence is too limited to calculate the potential size of the effect of early childhood programs on labor force participation rates or worker performance. However, we would expect the magnitude of such effects on the labor market to depend upon the size of the implicit child care subsidy (e.g., the subsidy would be 100 percent for full-time programs made available to families without charge) and the share of the population of workers with young children covered by the subsidy. In other words, a program that required families to pay more of the costs, one that provided only part-time care, or one that served a more targeted population would have a smaller effect than one with the opposite characteristics.

Macroeconomic Benefits

In addition to providing potential benefits for current workers with young children and for their employers, early childhood interventions represent an investment in the future workforce. The benefit-costs analyses reviewed in the previous section generally accounted for the private returns from this investment in the form of higher earnings in adulthood because of the expected increase in educational attainment. Some of the public returns associated with improved educational levels, such as higher taxes paid and lower levels of crime and welfare use, were also evaluated in the benefit-cost studies. However, a more educated future workforce also has the potential to generate improved macroeconomic outcomes as well. Notably, a sizable research base quantifies the link between the level and growth of an economy's human capital (often measured by education levels) and the rate of economic growth (see Krueger and Lindahl, 2001, for a recent review). Other evidence suggests that it is not just years of schooling that affect economic growth but the quality of school as well, as measured, for example, by math and science test scores (Hanushek and Kimko, 2000). Although economists have competing theories to explain this relationship and empirical estimates vary, quantitative studies suggest that education can have a large effect on economic growth (DeLong, Goldin, and Katz, 2003).

A related benefit is that a more educated, more skilled workforce can strengthen the competitive position of the U.S. economy in an increasingly competitive global marketplace. Technological change, coupled with globalization, has placed an increasing premium on more-educated workers, and the ability of the U.S. economy to remain competitive rests with the human capital of the workforce (Karoly and Panis, 2004). The future knowledge-based economy will value such skills as abstract reasoning, problem solving, communication, and collaboration. Investments in early childhood interventions, to the extent that they raise eventual educational attainment and other measures of skills that are valued in the workplace, can help raise the overall skill level in the economy and contribute to the economic success of the United States.

Noneconomic Benefits

To the extent that early childhood intervention programs generate the longer-term benefits documented in studies reviewed in this and earlier chapters, they may also generate broader benefits to society. Notably, economic and social inequalities have been increasing in recent decades. Economic disparities have been manifested in a widening gap between lower- and higher-wage workers and in the growth in income and wealth disparities for families (Burtless and Jencks, 2003). Such disparities are also evident in the gaps in outcomes across race and ethnic groups or across families defined by the education level of the family head. Rising economic inequality has implications for social disparities in such areas as family functioning, neighborhood quality, education, health, crime, and political participation (Neckerman, 2004). The strong relationship between these economic and social outcomes and education levels suggests that programs that narrow educational gaps will have collateral benefits in terms of reducing economic and social disparities, both overall and among various demographic subgroups.

Strengths and Limitations of Economic Evidence

Early childhood interventions have the potential to generate spillover benefits to the government and the rest of society that can be expressed in dollar terms and summed across various categories of benefits. Such benefits can then be compared with program costs to determine whether investments in early childhood programs can pay off in terms of shorter-term or longer-term benefits to various stakeholders. The review of evidence from benefit-cost studies presented in this chapter indicates that it is possible, in practice, for early childhood interventions to generate benefit streams that exceed the initial program costs.

This evidence is based on rigorous evaluations of a subset of early childhood programs and the associated studies that employ accepted methods of benefit-cost analysis for social programs. Early childhood interventions with favorable estimates of net benefits and benefit-cost ratios include home visiting/parent education programs and center-based ECE programs, including those that also include home visiting or parent education. Such favorable economic returns have been shown not only for smaller-scale demonstration programs but also for larger scale, real-world programs. The evidence of the economic returns from investing in early childhood interventions is particularly strong for programs that have long-term follow-up of program participants, measure a broad array of outcomes, and serve a more targeted population. The estimated benefits, even when they exceed program costs, can generally be viewed as conservative given limitations in the information available to predict benefits across the full range of potential favorable outcomes, especially in studies with short-term follow-up. The results of the studies reviewed here are also conservative in that they do not account for the other potential economic and noneconomic benefits typically not captured in benefit-cost studies, such as economy-wide benefits to the labor force and the macroeconomy.

The strength of the empirical evidence on the economic returns from early childhood investments has led some economists and others to frame such programs in the context of economic development (Rolnick and Grunewald, 2003; CED, 2004; Schweke, 2004). Traditional vehicles for state and local economic development funds include investments in infrastructure, business assistance, and workforce education and training. However, there is little empirical evidence to suggest that many of these activities generate positive net economic benefits for society as a whole. In some cases, jobs are exported from one community to another, so the total gain is zero. In other cases, jobs would have increased even without state and local economic development assistance, or the expected economic effect fails to materialize (Peters and Fisher, 2002; CED, 2004). In contrast, the favorable economic returns from early childhood interventions suggest they can be a worthwhile public-sector investment with a positive payoff to society as a whole.

Although the evidence of the economic benefits from early childhood interventions is compelling, it is important to recognize the limitations of the evidence base. Our analysis of the benefits and costs of early childhood programs in this chapter is based on a small number of programs with high-quality evaluations. While the results demonstrate that an economic payoff is possible, they do not suggest that such a payoff will exist for all early childhood interventions. In some cases, the favorable effects found for small-scale model programs may be attenuated when programs operate on a larger scale. The economic payoff may also be smaller when programs serve a broader population that does not stand to benefit to the same extent as more disadvantaged children served in targeted programs. In addition, new program models that have not been evaluated may, in fact, be ineffective. For example, programs that invest too few resources or that use resources in an ineffective manner may generate little in the way of improvement for participating children and their families.[13] Consequently, any economic benefit would be small or nonexistent. Thus, it is important to continue to assess early childhood programs in terms of their effects on the short- and long-term outcomes of participating children and their families and to translate those improvements into economic benefits that can be compared with program costs.

---

[13] For example, the CCDP proved ineffective, at least based on follow-up to age 5.

CHAPTER FIVE

Conclusions

The preceding chapters have addressed a range of issues related to investing in the lives of children prior to school entry, particularly for children at risk of adverse developmental outcomes. In this concluding chapter, we distill our synthesis of the research literature into a series of key results about early childhood interventions. In highlighting these results, we also point to important caveats and limits of our knowledge base.

The period from birth to age 5 is one of opportunity and vulnerability for healthy physical, emotional, social, and cognitive development.

Human development is the result of the complex interplay among genetic endowments and environmental conditions. Both nature and nurture play key roles—alone, and in interaction with one another—throughout the life course. The first few years of life, however, represent a particularly sensitive period in the process of development, a period of tremendous opportunity as well as vulnerability. Starting in the prenatal period and continuing until kindergarten entry, children progress through various developmental milestones associated with healthy development that have implications for cognitive functioning; behavioral, social, and self-regulatory capacities; and physical health. Subsequent development builds upon these early capacities, so they provide an important foundation for future success in school and beyond.

A variety of factors can provide critical support of healthy child development during these early years, or they may compromise the desired outcomes. They include the nature of early relationships with parents and other caregivers, the extent of cognitive stimulation, and access to adequate nutrition, health care, and other resources such as a safe home and neighborhood environment. Some children will be resilient in the face of various stressors in early childhood, while healthy development will be compromised for others, whether temporarily or more long-lasting.

A sizable fraction of children face risks that have the potential to limit their development in the years prior to school entry.

A number of factors have been associated with risks of developmental delay and longer-term adverse outcomes. Living in poverty is one such factor that affects 20 percent of children under age 6, or 4.7 million children overall: more than 50 percent of children living in a female-headed household, 40 percent of African-American children, and 33 percent of Latino children.[1] Independent of poverty status, children in single-parent families are at greater risk, along with those whose mothers have less than a high school education. Smaller, but still sizable, numbers of children are potentially at risk due to low birthweight, limited use of preventive health care, and living in high-risk neighborhoods and linguistically isolated households. Almost 50 percent of U.S. kindergarten children in a recent cohort examined as part of the ECLS-K faced at least one of four risk factors (mother is a high school dropout, family receives welfare or food stamps, single-parent household, and parents whose primary language is not English). Sixteen percent had two or more risk factors.

Exposure to these various sources of risk does not lead, with certainty, to adverse outcomes in early childhood and beyond. For some children, various protective factors will provide them with the resilience to advance along a positive trajectory despite facing one or more risks that may challenge healthy development. Other children ex-

---

[1] Welfare receipt is a related indicator of low family income.

posed to risk factors will not be as resilient, and the consequences during later periods of childhood and beyond can be considerable.

Variations in early childhood experiences are manifested in disparities in school readiness measures, and these gaps often persist as children age.

Disadvantages in early childhood have implications for how prepared children are when they enter school. School readiness is a multidimensional concept that captures not only cognitive skills but also those associated with socialization, self-regulatory behavior, and learning approaches. For the ECLS-K cohort, various assessments indicate that children with more disadvantaged backgrounds enter school with lower levels of the knowledge and social competencies that are important for subsequent school success. When entering kindergartners are assessed in terms of their pre-reading and numeracy skills, pro-social behaviors, behavior problems, and readiness to learn, one of the sharpest contrasts that emerges is between children differentiated by mother's education level. While these readiness measures indicate that children from more-enriched environments enter school better prepared, longitudinal data demonstrate that these early gaps persist and even widen as children progress through school. Thus, disadvantaged children do not advance at the same rate as their more-advantaged peers, so that achievement gaps tend to widen over time.

These achievement gaps are also manifested in the high proportion of disadvantaged children who do not meet basic proficiency standards in core subjects as they move through school. About 1 in 2 8th graders whose parents have less than a high school education do not demonstrate even partial mastery of fundamental reading or mathematics skills. By comparison, for students the same age whose parents have a college education, the fraction is about 1 in 20. The incidence of other undesirable outcomes, such as special education use, grade repetition, and dropping out of high school, is also higher for more-disadvantaged children. Low rates of school achievement are then associated with higher rates of undesirable outcomes in adulthood, such as being disconnected from school or work; welfare dependency; and delinquency, crime, and imprisonment. Although there is not a perfect causal link among early childhood experiences, the extent of school readiness, and unfavorable outcomes in the transition to adulthood, the risk factors that can compromise early development often lead to poor school performance and in turn to the adverse outcomes cited above. Even if only a portion of these detrimental outcomes in childhood and adulthood can be averted, the benefits may be substantial.

Early childhood intervention programs are designed to counteract various stressors in early childhood and promote healthy development.

Early childhood interventions are designed to provide a protective influence to compensate for the risk factors that potentially compromise healthy child development in the years before school entry. The protective influence may take the form of additional supports for the parents, children, or family as a unit that can affect a child directly through structured experiences or indirectly by enhancing the caregiving environment. While they share a common objective, early childhood interventions are extremely varied in their methods and there is no uniform model or approach. Key dimensions along which programs vary include

- the goals of the program in terms of outcomes the program aims to improve
- whether the child, the parent, or the parent-child dyad is the target of intervention
- the criteria defining the target population, e.g., low socioeconomic status, single parenthood
- the time span from the prenatal period to age 5 over which the intervention occurs; the types of services included, where they are provided, and the intensity with which they are delivered
- the extent of individualized attention
- the program's geographic reach.

Many of the program dimensions are dictated by the program goals and the underlying theory of how child and family behaviors can be changed by various environmental influences.

Rigorous evaluations of early childhood interventions can inform our understanding of the array of outcomes at school entry and beyond that programs may improve.

Although we may expect early childhood programs to produce beneficial effects based on underlying theories and knowledge of the complexities of early child development, a scientifically sound evaluation is required to know whether that promise holds in reality. The range of outcomes affected and the magnitudes of the effects are both of interest. The variation in early childhood intervention approaches suggests that such evaluations are needed for the full range of program models, ideally with the ability to ascertain the effects of varying key program features.

The best evaluation designs are those that provide the highest confidence that effects attributed to the program are indeed the result of the intervention, rather than some other influential factor or factors. A randomized experiment, when implemented properly, is considered the gold standard for investigating the causal effect of an intervention on the participants. Such designs are not always feasible, so researchers may apply quasi-experimental methods as an alternative to an experimental design. In the absence of experimental conditions, such approaches may have weaknesses that compromise the ability to draw inferences about the true causal effect of a given intervention.

While many early childhood interventions have been implemented, and a subset of those have been evaluated in some fashion, only a relatively small subset have been evaluated using scientifically sound methods. Our review of the literature identified published evaluations for 20 early childhood programs with well-implemented experimental designs or strong quasi-experimental designs. These programs all serve children or their families from the prenatal period to age 5, with a child development focus and assessment of program impacts for child-specific outcomes. We excluded programs implemented outside the United States or before 1960, as well as those designed to primarily serve children with special needs. Some programs were excluded because their evaluations did not meet a set of minimum standards for scientific rigor (e.g., large enough sample size). Sixteen of the 20 programs have the strongest evidence base because they identify effects at the time of school entry or beyond. This group included both effective and ineffective programs based on the statistical significance of estimated program effects. The remaining four programs have a promising evidence base and evidence of favorable effects, although they rely on measures of outcomes for children as young as 2 or 3.

Rigorous scientific research has demonstrated that early childhood interventions can improve the lives of participating children and families in both the short run and longer run.

We examined the following benefit domains: cognition and academic achievement, behavioral and emotional competencies, educational progression and attainment, child maltreatment, health, delinquency and crime, social welfare program use, and labor market success. For each of these domains (with the exception of social welfare program use), statistically significant benefits were found in at least two out of every three programs we reviewed that measured outcomes in that domain.[2] In some cases, the improved outcomes in these domains were demonstrated soon after the program ended; in other cases, the favorable effects were observed through adolescence and in the transition to adulthood. In one case, lasting benefits were measured 35 years after the intervention ended. Even though there is evidence that early benefits in terms of cognition or school achievement may eventually fade, the evidence indicates that there can be longer-lasting gains in educational progress and attainment, labor market outcomes, dependency, and pro-social behaviors. In addition, a few studies indicate that the parents of participating children can also benefit from

---

[2] In the case of social services use in adulthood, this outcome was measured in only two of the five programs that measured effects in adulthood. The outcome was significant in only one of the two programs with this measure.

early intervention programs, particularly when they are specifically targeted by the intervention.

The magnitudes of the favorable effects can often be sizable. The size of the effects tend to be more modest for cognitive and behavioral measures, and, as noted, the favorable gains in these measures often shrink in size over time. The effects are more substantial and long-lasting for such outcomes as special education placement and grade retention, as well as some of the other outcomes in adolescence and adulthood. At the same time, it is important to note that the improved outcomes realized by participants in targeted early intervention programs are typically not large enough to fully compensate for the disadvantages they face. For example, IQ and educational achievement scores, prevalence of grade repetition, use of special education, high school graduation rates, and contacts with the criminal justice system are all less favorable for intervention participants, even after the intervention, than they are for more-advantaged, nonparticipating children of similar age. Thus, while early intervention programs can improve outcomes over what they otherwise would have been, they typically do not fully close the gap between the disadvantaged children they serve and their more-advantaged peers.

Although the evaluations of these 20 programs can demonstrate their effectiveness in terms of improving outcomes for participating children and their families, they do not represent all early childhood programs, or even the subset of effective programs. Moreover, evidence of the effectiveness of a given program does not imply that all similar programs will have the same effect or that even the same program implemented under different conditions will have the same effects. Ultimately, program effects may vary due to a variety of factors, including program design, the population served, and the local context in which a program is delivered.

A very limited evidence base points to several program features that may be associated with better outcomes for children: better-trained caregivers, smaller child-to-staff ratios, and greater intensity of services.

The early intervention research literature has rarely formally evaluated the differential effect of varying key program features. While there are a few exceptions, our inferences about what makes for successful interventions are drawn from experimental and quasi-experimental evaluations of program design features, as well as comparisons of effects across model programs based on variation in program features. As part of this study, we undertook one such analysis that considered variation in outcomes associated with program type. Such an analysis is limited, however, by the small amount of variation across program models with rigorous evaluations. Nevertheless, the evidence from this analysis, combined with what we know from formal evaluations of variation in program features and other meta-analyses, suggests three features in particular that may be associated with more effective programs.

First, programs with better-trained caregivers appear to be more effective. In center-based programs, this may take the form of a lead teacher with a college degree as opposed to no degree. In home visiting programs, researchers have found stronger effects when services are delivered by trained nurses as opposed to paraprofessional or lay professional home visitors. Second, for center-based programs, there is evidence to suggest that programs are more successful when they have smaller child-to-staff ratios. Third, there is some evidence that more-intensive programs are associated with better outcomes, although we are not able to definitively indicate, for example, the optimal number of program hours and how they vary by child characteristics. It is likely that some minimum level of program hours is required to improve outcomes, but that at some point the benefits from additional hours may be less than what is gained from the initial level.

It is noteworthy that the features associated with more successful programs are costly. Thus, it appears that more money may need to be spent to obtain larger effects. At the same time, there may be thresholds after which diminishing marginal returns set in. The optimal intensity of early childhood interventions and the timing of those interventions for different subgroups of children defined by various risk levels remain to be determined by further research.

The favorable effects of early childhood programs can translate into dollar benefits for the government, participants, and other members of society.

Depending on the range and intensity of services delivered, early childhood interventions may range in cost from modest to a considerable financial investment. It is therefore reasonable to ask whether the costs can be justified in terms of the benefits associated with the range of favorable effects demonstrated by such programs. Indeed, many of the outcomes that early childhood programs improve may generate benefits that can be translated into dollar figures, aggregated across benefit categories, and compared with program costs.

For example, if school outcomes improve, there may be fewer resources spent on remedial education services in the form of repeated grades or special education classes. If improvements in school performance lead to higher educational attainment and subsequent economic success in adulthood, the government may benefit from higher tax revenues and reduced outlays for social welfare programs and the criminal justice system. As a result of improved economic outcomes, participants themselves benefit from higher lifetime incomes, and other members of society gain from reduced levels of delinquency and crime. If early childhood interventions also lead to improvements in parental outcomes such as parents' own educational attainment, labor force outcomes, use of social welfare programs, or criminal activity, additional dollar benefits will flow to the government, participants, and other members of society.

Although a subset of the improved outcomes associated with early childhood interventions cannot be readily translated into dollar benefits (this is the case, for example, with measures of cognitive development, pro-social behaviors, or behavior problems), benefit-cost analysis can be used to aggregate the dollar benefits associated with those outcomes that can be expressed in monetary terms and then to compare total benefits with total costs. Such comparisons are made taking account of the time path of costs and benefits (i.e., an upfront cost associated with the program followed by benefits that may accrue in the near term or farther into the future). Benefits and costs can also be viewed from the perspective of various stakeholders, such as the public sector (i.e., the government or collectively members of society as taxpayers) and components of the private sector, namely the program participants themselves or other members of society who were not program participants.

Economic analyses of several early childhood interventions demonstrate that effective programs can repay the initial investment with savings to government and benefits to society down the road.

When early childhood programs are effective—in other words, when they have significant and meaningful effects on outcomes for participating children and families—our analysis in Chapter Four shows that it is possible for the dollar benefits associated with the favorable effects to exceed program costs. Evidence that early childhood interventions can be justified on economic terms comes from a subset of the 20 interventions we reviewed. In particular, one or more benefit-cost analyses have been conducted for seven of the 20 programs, while another study provides two other benefit-cost analyses based on a meta-analysis of home visiting programs for at-risk children and a meta-analysis of early childhood education programs for low-income three- and four-year olds. These benefit-cost studies rely on the results of the rigorous outcome evaluations of these programs and accepted methods for benefit-cost analysis. Although results across programs are not strictly comparable because of differences in methodology, they can demonstrate whether, in principle, early childhood interventions can generate benefits that outweigh the program costs.

The benefit-cost studies showed that two programs (CCDP and IHDP) were unable to exhibit positive net benefits to society as a whole. In one case, the program was not effective, so there were no substantial improvements that could lead to dollar savings. In the other case, while the program had significant and favorable effects as of the last follow-up at age 8, none of the outcomes assessed could be translated into dollar savings. For the remaining studies with positive net benefits, the estimates of net benefits per child served range from about $1,400 to nearly $240,000. Viewed another way, the returns to society for each dollar invested extend from $1.26 to $17.07.

Positive net benefits were found for programs that required a large investment (e.g., the Abecedarian program with intensive services over five years that cost over $40,000 per child), as well as those that cost considerably less (e.g., HIPPY, which costs less than $2,000 per child). Programs with per-child costs within this range also generated positive net benefits. The economic returns were favorable for programs that focused on home visiting or parent education, as well as those that combined those services with early childhood education. The largest benefit-cost ratios were associated with programs having longer-term follow-up because they allowed measurement at older ages of such outcomes as educational attainment, delinquency and crime, earnings, and others that most readily translate into dollar benefits. Not only do the studies with measured improvements based on long-term follow-up demonstrate that the benefits from early interventions can be long-lasting, they also give more confidence that the savings the programs generate can be substantial. Programs with evaluations that have followed children only until school entry or a few years beyond typically do not measure those outcomes that are likely to be associated with the largest dollar benefits, although they may eventually generate large savings as well.

Limitations in translating the full range of benefits from early childhood interventions into dollar values means that most benefit-cost calculations of effective programs are likely to understate the dollar benefits, and hence estimates of net benefits and the benefit-cost ratio will be underestimated as well. Moreover, such analyses do not incorporate some of the other potential economic and non-economic benefits that may flow from effective early interventions. These include improved labor market performance for the parents of participating children and their employers, as well as stronger economic growth and competitiveness as a result of improvements in educational attainment and skills of the future workforce. Effective interventions may also produce a lessening of economic and social disparities, which may be valued by society as well.

The economic benefits of early childhood interventions are likely to be greatest for programs that effectively serve targeted, disadvantaged children compared with universal programs or programs that serve more-advantaged children.

From the benefit-cost analyses reviewed in Chapter Four, there is some evidence that the economic returns from investing in early intervention programs are larger when programs are effectively targeted. The strongest evidence in support of this conclusion comes from the benefit-cost analysis of the NFP home visiting program. In that study, the effects of the program were larger for a higher-risk sample of mothers. Consequently, the return for each dollar invested was $5.70 for the higher-risk population served compared with $1.26 for the lower-risk population. It is possible that another intervention program for the lower-risk population—one that is designed to provide a mix of services that would be most effective in meeting the needs of that group—would have a benefit-cost ratio equivalent to that found for the higher-risk group. This finding indicates that it is not reasonable to expect the returns reported in Chapter Four for specific programs serving specific disadvantaged populations to apply when the same program serves a different population.

While many early childhood interventions are designed to serve a targeted, disadvantaged population, others aim to provide services universally. The Oklahoma Pre-K program is one such example in our group of 20 programs. It has not yet been subject to a benefit-cost analysis. However, the findings presented here suggest that we would not expect to see the same returns measured for the Perry Preschool program or Chicago CPC program in a universal program. Hence, the benefit-cost ratio would be lower than what is measured for the targeted programs. The ratio for a universal program may still exceed 1, but it will indicate a lower return per dollar invested compared with a targeted program. However, a universal program may be justified on other grounds. For example, it may be less costly to administer because there is no requirement to determine eligibility (Barnett, Brown, and Shore, 2004). Universal programs also avoid the potential stigma associated with targeted programs and may receive broader support for public-sector funding.

In distilling our synthesis of the literature into these ten key findings, it is important to acknowledge that our conclusions rest on a solid, but still limited, evidence base. Although that evidence base can always be strengthened by further research and evaluation of early childhood intervention programs, our findings nevertheless indicate that a body of sound research exists to guide decisionmakers in making resource allocations. This research base helps to identify those children at greatest risk, the range of early intervention programs that have high-quality evaluations, the demonstrated benefits associated with programs that have been carefully studied, some of the key features associated with successful programs, and the economic benefits that can flow from devoting resources to effective programs. These proven results therefore signal the future promise of investing early in the lives of disadvantaged children.

Descriptions of Early Childhood Intervention Programs Included in the Study

Table A.1 provides a brief summary of the program features for each of the 20 early childhood intervention programs we study (Project CARE is counted as two program models), first for the 16 programs with a strong evidence base and then for the four programs with a promising evidence base. We also include the URL for those programs with Web sites that provide additional program information. Relevant citations that we relied on for the results presented in the study are listed as well.

Table A.1
Descriptions and Citations for Early Childhood Intervention Programs Included in the Study

Program	Description	Citations
	Programs with a Strong Evidence Base	
Carolina Abece-darian Project	The Carolina Abecedarian Project was a comprehensive early education program for young children at risk for developmental delays and school failure. The program operated in a single site in North Carolina between 1972 and 1985, and it involved both a preschool component and a school-age component. Children entered the program from infancy up to 6 months of age. The preschool program offered a full-day, year-round, center-based stimulating and structured environment, along with nutritional supplements, pediatric care, and social work services. http://www.fpg.unc.edu/~abc/	Ramey and Campbell (1984) Campbell and Ramey (1994) Ramey and Campbell (1994) Campbell and Ramey (1995) Campbell et al. (2002)
Chicago Child-Parent Centers (CPC)	The Chicago CPC program has been providing center-based preschool education to disadvantaged children in high-poverty Chicago neighborhoods since 1967. The centers operate during the school year through the Chicago public school system and are located in public elementary schools. The preschool provides a structured part-day program for children ages 3 and 4 that emphasizes a child-centered, individualized approach to social and cognitive development. The centers also require regular parental participation. Related program services continue after kindergarten entry and through grades 1, 2, or 3. http://www.waisman.wisc.edu/cls/Program.htm.	Reynolds (1994) Reynolds (1995) Reynolds and Temple (1995) Reynolds (1997) Reynolds, Chang, and Temple (1997) Reynolds and Temple (1998) Reynolds (2000) Reynolds et al. (2001) Reynolds et al. (2002)
Comprehensive Child Development Program (CCDP)	The CCDP aimed to enhance child development and help low-income families to achieve economic self-sufficiency. The program initially began in 1988 with 22 sites that operated for five years; two more sites started in 1990. The program was designed to serve families from as early as the prenatal period through age 5, although in practice wide variation in implementation length was observed between sites. CCDP projects were designed to build upon existing service delivery networks and relied on case managers to coordinate the service needs of a group of families. Case managers provided some services directly (e.g., counseling, life skills	St. Pierre et al. (1997)

Table A.1—continued

Program	Description	Citations
	training), and provided access to other services such as immunizations, childcare, and prenatal care through referrals and brokered arrangements.	
DARE to be You	DARE to be You is a multilevel prevention program, operating in several sites in Colorado, that targets parents of two- to five-year-olds in high-risk families. The center-based program focuses on parenting skills, and the aspects that contribute to youth's resiliency to substance abuse later in life, such as parents' self efficacy, effective child rearing, social support, problem-solving skills, and children's developmental attainments. The program offers 15 to 18 hours of parent training workshops and concurrent children's programs, preferably in a 10- to 12-week period. Other program elements include training for child care providers and training for social service agency workers who work with families. http://www.coopext.colostate.edu/DTBY/index.html	Miller-Heyl, MacPhee, and Fritz (1998)
Early Training Project (ETP)	The ETP was a demonstration project that served a cohort of children born in 1958. The program, implemented in Murfreesboro, Tennessee, was designed to improve the educability of young children from low-income homes. The program consisted of a ten-week summer preschool program for the two or three summers prior to first grade, and weekly home visits during the remainder of the year.	Gray and Klaus (1970) Gray and Ramsey (1982) Gray, Ramsey, and Klaus (1982) Lazar and Darlington (1982)
Head Start	Head Start is a federally funded community-based preschool program initiated in the 1960s with an overall goal of increasing the school readiness of eligible young children ages 3 to 5 in low-income families. Head Start preschools, operating either part- or full-day, provide a range of services, including early childhood education, nutrition and health services, and parent education and involvement. There is no single Head Start program model and programs exist in all 50 states. http://www2.acf.dhhs.gov/programs/hsb/	Currie and Thomas (1995) Currie and Thomas (1999) Aughinbaugh (2001) Garces, Thomas, and Currie (2002) Abbott-Shim, Lambert, and McCarty (2003)

Table A.1—continued

Program	Description	Citations
High/Scope Perry Preschool Project	The High/Scope Perry Preschool Project was a center-based early childhood education program designed to promote children's intellectual, social, and emotional learning and development. The program was conducted from 1962 to 1967 in Ypsilanti, Michigan, and targeted three- and four-year-old African-American children who were living in poverty and had low IQ scores. The school-year program emphasized learning through active and direct child-initiated experiences rather than through directed teaching. Teachers conducted part-day, daily classroom sessions for children and weekly home visits. http://www.highscope.org	Weikart, Bond, and McNeil (1978) Schweinhart and Weikart (1980) Berrueta-Clement et al. (1984) Schweinhart, Barnes, and Weikart (1993) Schweinhart (2004) Schweinhart et al. (2005)
HIPPY (Home Instruction Program for Preschool Youngsters) USA	HIPPY is a two-year parent involvement program that offers home-based early childhood education for three-, four-, and five-year-old children. The program targets parents with limited formal education from economically disadvantaged families. HIPPY helps parents enhance their children's school readiness, through the use of a structured curriculum and books and materials designed to strengthen children's cognitive skills, early literacy skills, social/emotional development, and physical development. The program is designed so that mothers deliver the HIPPY lessons to their children daily, with support in the form of biweekly home visits from a paraprofessional and biweekly group meetings with paraprofessionals and other parents. HIPPY is an international program that started in Israel in 1969 and has been in operation in the U.S. since 1984 with programs in 26 states. http://www.hippyusa.org	Baker, Piotrkowski, Brook-Gunn, (1998)
Houston Parent-Child Development Center (PCDC)	The Houston PCDC was a two-year parent-child education program for children ages 1 to 3, whose goal was preventing behavior problems in young children. The program was implemented from 1970 to 1972 and targeted low-income Mexican American families that lived in Houston barrios. The first year of the program involved biweekly home visits to the mother and child by paraprofessional educators,	Johnson et al. (1974) Johnson and Breckenridge (1982) Johnson and Walker (1991)

Table A.1—continued

Program	Description	Citations
	several weekend sessions for entire families, English language classes for the mothers, a medical examination of the child, and referrals to community resources. In the second year, mothers and children attended PCDC activities for up to four mornings a week, along with evening sessions that included fathers, and a continuation of language classes and community services.	
Incredible Years	The Incredible Years series is a set of comprehensive curricula for children ages 2 to 8 and their parents and teachers. It targets high-risk children or children displaying behavior problems. The curricula are designed to work jointly to promote emotional and social competence and to prevent, reduce, and treat children's behavioral and emotional problems. The Incredible Years parent-training involves 12 to 14 weekly sessions, emphasizing such parenting skills as how to set limits, how to play with children, and how to handle misbehavior, and incorporates videotaped scenes to encourage group discussion and problem solving. The child-training program uses a small-group curriculum for children exhibiting conduct problems, and is offered in weekly sessions for 18 to 20 weeks. The Incredible Years has been in operation since 1980 in multiple sites in the U.S., as well as sites in Canada, the UK, and Sweden. http://www.incredibleyears.com/	Webster-Stratton, Kolpacoff, and Hollinsowth (1988) Webster-Stratton (1998) Webster-Stratton, Reid, and Hammond (2001)
Infant Health and Development Program (IHDP)	The IHDP was a comprehensive intervention consisting of early child development programs and family support services tailored to reduce the prevalence of health and developmental problems among low-birthweight, premature infants. Targeting infants upon discharge from the neonatal nursery until 36 months of age, the program provided home visiting, parent group meetings, and a center-based child development program for children. The program operated in eight medical institutions throughout the U.S. from 1985 to 1988.	IHDP (1990) McCormick et al. (1991) Ramey et al. (1992) McCormick et al. (1993) Brooks-Gunn, McCarton, et al. (1994) Brooks-Gunn, McCormick, et al. (1994) McCarton et al. (1997) Hill, Brooks-Gunn, and Waldfogel (2003)

Table A.1—continued

Program	Description	Citations
Nurse-Family Partnership (NFP) Program	The NFP (formerly Prenatal/Early Infancy Home Visitation by Nurses) provides intensive and comprehensive home visitation by public health nurses to low-income first-time pregnant women and mothers of any age. The visits begin during pregnancy and continue through the child's second birthday and are intended to help women improve their prenatal health and the outcomes of pregnancy; improve the care provided to infants and toddlers; and improve women's own personal development. The NFP program has been evaluated in trials in Elmira, New York; Memphis, Tennessee; and Denver, Colorado. More recently, the program has been replicated in 23 states across the U.S. http://www.nccfc.org/nurseFamilyPartnership.cfm	Olds, Henderson, Chamberlin, et al. (1986) Olds, Henderson, Tatelbaum, et al. (1986) Olds et al. (1988) Olds, Henderson, and Kitzman (1994) Olds (1996) Olds, Eckenrode, et al. (1997) Olds, Kitzman, et al. (1997) Olds et al. (2002) Olds, Kitzman, et al. (2004) Olds, Robinson, et al. (2004)
Oklahoma Pre-K	Since 1998, the state of Oklahoma has offered a voluntary, one-year free pre-kindergarten program to all four-year-old students in participating school districts. Pre-K teachers are required to hold a bachelor's degree as well as early childhood certification. The program also imposes restrictions on class size (20 students) and child-teacher ratios (10 to 1). http://www.sde.state.ok.us	Gormley and Gayer (forthcoming) Gormley et al. (forthcoming)
Project CARE (Carolina Approach to Responsive Education)— two models	Project CARE was a longitudinal early intervention study that targeted families whose infants were at elevated risk for delayed development. Participants were subject to either of two interventions or a control group. The interventions consisted of either a family-focused home visiting program that provided general family support, or home visits in addition to child attendance at an educational development center that utilized a structured curriculum. Home visits began in the month after the child's birth, and children assigned to the	Ramey et al. (1985) Wasik et al. (1990)

Table A.1—continued

Program	Description	Citations
	educational development center began attending at some point between 6 weeks and 3 months of age. Both interventions continued until age 5. Project CARE was implemented in North Carolina between 1978 and 1983.	
Syracuse Family Development Research Program (FDRP)	The FDRP was a comprehensive early childhood program designed to improve child and family functioning. The program operated in a single site in Syracuse, New York, between 1969 and 1976. The FDRP targeted young, African-American, single, low-income mothers who were in the last trimester of their first or second pregnancy. The program provided weekly home visits by paraprofessionals, parent training, individualized day care, and structured preschool. Services began prenatally and lasted until children reached elementary school age.	Honig and Lally (1982) Lally, Mangione, and Honig (1988)

Programs with a Promising Evidence Base

Program	Description	Citations
Developmentally Supportive Care: Newborn Individualized Developmental Care and Assessment Progra (DSC/NIDCAP)	The NIDCAP focuses on the needs of infants in neonatal intensive care units (NICUs). It is a relationship-based and family-centered program that relies on neurobehavioral observation to develop an in-depth behavioral developmental profile of preterm low-birthweight infants. NIDCAP encourages parents and other key family members to be constantly present in the NICU and to take charge of the development and nurturing of their infants. Biweekly visits are provided to families post-release from the NICU, up until the child reaches age 2. Comprehensive training is also provided to developmental specialists, nurse educators, a multidisciplinary leadership support team, nursing staff, and a parent council. Eleven NIDCAP training centers, including ten across the U.S. and one in Europe, provide consultation and training for successful delivery of the program. http://www.nidcap.org	Resnick et al. (1987) Becker et al. (1991)
Early Head Start	Early Head Start is a federally funded community-based program that provides child and family development services to low-income pregnant women and families with infants and toddlers up to age 3. The program uses multiple strategies, including home visiting, case management, child	Love et al. (2002a) Love et al. (2002b) Roggman et al. (2002)

Table A.1—continued

Program	Description	Citations
	development, parenting education, nutrition education, child care, health care and referrals, and family support. Early Head Start was first implemented in1994 and has been operated in hundreds of sites across the U.S. No single program model exists, and each site selects delivery options that will best meet the needs of the families and communities it serves. http://www.acf.hhs.gov/programs/hsb/programs/ehs/ehs2.htm	
Parents As Teachers	Parents as Teachers is a voluntary early childhood parent education and family support program that begins at or before the birth of the child and continues until kindergarten entry. Program services include home visits to families, developmental screenings of children, parent group meetings, and a resource network that links families with needed community resources. The Parents as Teachers program was created in 1981 and is a universal access model adaptable for families from all types of communities. http://www.patnc.org	Wagner, Cameto, and Gerlach-Downie (1996) Wagner et al. (1999) Wagner and Clayton (1999) Wagner, Iida et al. (2001) Wagner, Spiker, et al. (2001)
Reach Out and Read	Reach Out and Read is a national program that promotes reading aloud to young at-risk children by using the pediatric office as a site for education and intervention. Doctors and nurses give new books to children at each well-child visit from 6 months of age to 5 years and accompany these books with developmentally appropriate advice to parents about reading aloud with their child. First implemented in 1989, Reach Out and Read is available in all 50 states, the District of Columbia, Puerto Rico, and Guam. http://www.reachoutandread.org	Golova et al. (1999) High et al. (2000)

Methodology for the Analysis of Cognitive Outcomes in Chapter Three

This appendix describes the methods used to estimate the results presented in Table 3.7. The goal of the analysis was to determine whether programs that offered only home visiting/parent education obtained systematically different child outcomes from programs that offered a combination of home visiting/parent education and ECE services. Note that the latter type of program generally offered more-intensive services in terms of the total number of hours of treatment the family would receive while participating.

Due to data limitations, we could undertake this exercise only for cognitive outcomes. As shown in Table 3.1, very few programs measured results in the crime, health, and child maltreatment domains. More programs measured outcomes related to education and behavioral and social well-being, but still not enough to enable a useful statistical comparison between the two types of programs.

The analysis used the first achievement or IQ test result available for each program at approximately age 5 or 6. We selected this age because we wanted to focus on the school readiness aspects of the program effects. When results for an overall achievement measure were available, we used that. When only subject-specific achievement measures were available, we used the reading score. For the programs designated as having a promising evidence base because they did not follow study children to school-entry or beyond, we used the achievement test score at the oldest age available, which was generally around age 3.

We collected 15 IQ or achievement scores from the 20 programs included in this study, and then converted these results into a standardized effect size, so that the results from different studies could be directly compared. When the means for the control and treatment groups were reported, we computed the effect size by dividing the difference between the means for the treatment and control groups by the pooled standard deviation of that mean. Specifically, we calculated Cohen's d as:

$$d = \frac{\bar{Y}_t - \bar{Y}_c}{s_p} \ ,$$

where

$$s_p = \sqrt{\frac{s_t + s_c}{2}} \ .$$

In this formulation, $\bar{Y}_t$ and $\bar{Y}_c$ equal the treatment and control group means, respectively, and s_p is the pooled standard deviation calculated from the treatment and control group standard deviations, s_t and s_c, respectively.

Furthermore, we adjusted these effect sizes to account for possible biases inherent in small samples as recommended by Hedges (1981) (see Lipsey and Wilson, 2001, pp. 48–49). In some cases when the mean was not available, we computed the effect size using information such as the mean difference and the p-value of a test that the two means were different (see Lipsey and Wilson, 2001, for information about these methods).

After converting results from each program into a standardized effect size, we sorted the programs into one of two approaches using the taxonomy we developed in Chapter Two: home visiting/parent education only and "combination" programs that provide home visiting/parent education combined with ECE. One program in our set of 20 did not fall into either of these approaches (see Figure 2.2).

The Oklahoma Pre-K program is strictly an early childhood education program, so we did not include results from this program in the analysis.

The raw data used in the analysis are reported in Table B.1 (see also Figure 3.1), including the four programs with missing data. As this table shows, among the programs with data, six are in the home visiting/parent education approach and the other nine programs are in the "combination" approach.[1]

We estimated a pooled effect size obtained from random-effect meta-analysis for the two program approaches. The estimated effect size for the home visiting/parent education programs is 0.212, 0.113 lower than the estimated effect size of 0.325 for the combination programs. A meta-analysis regression test of the difference in effect size between the combination and other programs was statistically significant at only the 0.40 level, indicating no difference between the estimated effect size of these two program approaches.

We performed a number of sensitivity analyses. We estimated the meta-analysis regression excluding the CCDP results as a way to address the concerns that have been raised regarding the implementation and evaluation of that program. We also estimated the regression excluding the only quasi-experimental evaluation among the 15 studies—the CPC program. In addition, the model was estimated excluding Read Out and Read and DARE to be You because their cognitive score measures were least similar to those of the other programs; hence, it is possible that the effect sizes are less comparable as well. The Houston PCDC program also stands out for the late age of test measurement (age 9.5), so we tested the sensitivity of the results to the exclusion of that program as well. In each case, the mean effect size for "combination" programs did not change substantively with the exclusion of these programs, and the regression coefficient testing the difference in program approaches was not significant when these

---

[1] Note that some of the programs that had statistically significant findings for cognitive outcomes in Table 3.1 may not have a statistically significant outcome in Table B.1 because of the way outcomes were selected for inclusion in the meta-analysis.

four evaluations were separately omitted from the sample or when age of score measurement was controlled for in the model.

Table B.1
Data Used in Analysis of Cognitive Outcomes

Program	Mean Adjusted Effect Size (Cognitive Outcome)
Home Visiting/Parent Education	
NFP	0.18*
DSC/NIDCAP	a__
Parents as Teachers	0.06
Project CARE (no ECE)	–0.49+
HIPPY USA	0.24
Reach Out and Read	0.69***
DARE to be You	0.37**
Incredible Years	a__
"Combination" (Home Visiting/Parent Education and Early Childhood Education)	
Early Head Start	0.10*
Syracuse FDRP	a__
CCDP	–0.06
IHDP	0.02
Project CARE (with ECE)	0.71*
Abecedarian	0.62*
Houston PCDC	0.52*
ETP	0.60+
Perry Preschool	0.97**
Chicago CPC	0.35**
Head Start	a__

SOURCE: Authors calculations based on sources cited in Appendix A.
NOTES: See Table 2.2 for full program names.
+ p < 0.10; * p < 0.05; ** p < 0.01; *** p < 0.001.
a No cognitive measure available.

References

Abbott-Shim, Martha, Richard Lambert, and Frances McCarty, "A Comparison of School Readiness Outcomes for Children Randomly Assigned to a Head Start Program and the Program's Wait List," *Journal of Education for Students Placed at Risk*, Vol. 8, No. 2, 2003, pp. 191–214.

Anderson, Patricia M., and Philip B. Levine, "Child Care and Mothers' Employment Decisions," in Rebecca M. Blank and David Card, eds., *Finding Jobs: Work and Welfare Reform*, New York, N.Y.: Russell Sage Foundation, 2000.

Aos, Steve, Roxanne Lieb, Jim Mayfield, Marna Miller, and Annie Pennucci, *Benefits and Costs of Prevention and Early Intervention Programs for Youth*, Olympia: Washington State Institute for Public Policy, September 17, 2004. Online at http://www.wsipp.wa.gov/rptfiles/04-07-3901.pdf and http://www.wsipp.wa.gov/rptfiles/04-07-3901a.pdf (as of July 8, 2005).

Aughinbaugh, Alison, "Does Head Start Yield Long-Term Benefits?" *Journal of Human Resources*, Vol. 36, No. 4, Autumn 2001, pp. 641–665.

Baker, Amy J. L., Chaya S. Piotrkowski, and Jeanne Brook-Gunn, "The Effects of the Home Instruction Program for Preschool Youngsters on Children's School Performance at the End of the Program and One Year Later," *Early Childhood Research Quarterly*, Vol. 13, No. 4, 1998, pp. 571–586.

Barnett, W. Steven, "Benefit-Cost Analysis of Preschool Education: Findings from a 25-Year Follow-Up," *American Journal of Orthopsychiatry*, Vol. 63, No. 4, 1993, pp. 500–508.

————, "Long-Term Effects of Early Childhood Programs on Cognitive and School Outcomes," *The Future of Children*, Vol. 5, 1995, pp. 25–50.

————, "Economics of Early Childhood Intervention," in Jack P. Shonkoff and Samuel J. Meisels, eds., *Handbook of Early Childhood Intervention*, 2nd edition, New York, N.Y.: Cambridge University Press, 2000.

Barnett, W. Steven, Clive R. Belfield, and Milgros Nores, "Lifetime Cost-Benefit Analysis," in Lawrence J. Schweinhart, Jeanne Montie, Zongping Xiang, W. Steven Barnett, Clive R. Belfield, and Milagros Nores, eds., *Lifetime Effects: The High/Scope Perry Preschool Study Through Age 40*, Monographs of the High/Scope Educational Research Foundation, 14, Ypsilanti, Mich.: High/Scope Press, 2005, pp. 130–157.

Barnett, W. Steven, Kirsty Brown, and Rima Shore, "The Universal vs. Targeted Debate: Should the United States Have Preschool for All?" *NIEER Preschool Policy Matters*, Issue 6, April 2004. Online at http://nieer.org/resources/policybriefs/6.pdf (as of July 8, 2005).

Becker, Patricia T., Patricia C. Grunwald, J. Randall Moorman, and Sherry Stuhr, "Outcomes of Developmentally Supportive Nursing Care for Very Low Birthweight Infants," *Nursing Research*, Vol. 40, No. 3, 1991, pp. 150–155.

Behrman, Richard E., Deanna S. Gomby, and Patti L. Culross, "Home Visiting: Recent Program Evaluations," *The Future of Children*, Vol. 9, No. 1, 1999.

Belfield, Clive R., *Early Childhood Education: How Important Are the Cost-Savings to the School System?* Center for Early Care and Education, February 2004a. Online at http://www.winningbeginningny.org/databank/documents/belfield_report_000.pdf (as of July 8, 2005).

————, *Investing in Early Childhood Education in Ohio: An Economic Appraisal, Report prepared for Renewing Our Schools, Securing Our Future: A National Task Force on Public Education*, Washington, D.C., August 2004b. Online at http://www.americanprogress.org/site/pp.asp?c=biJRJ8OVF&b=172214 (as of July 8, 2005).

————, "Intergenerational Impacts of Early Childhood Education," unpublished manuscript, 2005.

Berrueta-Clement, John R., Lawrence J. Schweinhart, W. Steven Barnett, et al., *Changed Lives: The Effects of the Perry Preschool Program on Youths*

Through Age 19, Monographs of the High/Scope Educational Research Foundation, 8, Ypsilanti, Mich.: High/Scope Press, 1984.

Blau, David M., *The Child Care Problem: An Economic Analysis,* New York, N.Y.: Russell Sage Foundation, 2001.

Blau, David M., and Janet Currie, "Preschool, Day Care, and Afterschool Care: Who's Minding the Kids?" University of North Carolina at Chapel Hill—Department of Economics and University of California, Los Angeles—Department of Economics, 2004. Online at http://papers.ssrn.com/sol3/papers.cfm?abstract_id=579207 (as of July 8, 2005).

Board on Children, Youth and Families, *Getting to Positive Outcomes for Children in Child Care—A Summary of Two Workshops,* Washington, D.C.: National Research Council and Institute of Medicine, 2001.

Braswell, James S., Anthony D. Lutkus, Wendy S. Grigg, Shari L. Santapau, Brenda S. Tay-Lim, and Matthew S. Johnson, *The Nation's Report Card: Mathematics 2000,* NCES 2001-517, Washington, D.C.: National Center for Education Statistics, U.S. Department of Education, 2001.

Brofenbrenner, Urie, *The Ecology of Human Development,* Cambridge, Mass.: Harvard University Press, 1979.

Brooks-Gunn, Jeanne, Lisa Berlin, and Allison Fuligni, "Early Childhood Intervention Programs: What About the Family?" in Jack P. Shonkoff and Samuel J. Meisels, eds., *Handbook of Early Childhood Intervention,* 2nd edition, New York, N.Y.: Cambridge University Press, 2000.

Brooks-Gunn, Jeanne, Cecilia M. McCarton, Patrick H. Casey, Marie C. McCormick, Charles R. Bauer, Judy C. Bernbaum, Jon Tyson, Mark Swanson, Forrest C. Bennett, David T. Scott, James Tonascia, and Curtis L. Meinert, "Early Intervention in Low-Birth-Weight Premature Infants: Results Through Age 5 Years from the Infant Health and Development Program," *Journal of the American Medical Association,* Vol. 272, No. 16, 1994, pp. 1257–1262.

Brooks-Gunn, Jeanne, Marie C. McCormick, Sam Shapiro, April Ann Benasich, and George W. Black, "The Effects of Early Education Intervention on Maternal Employment, Public Assistance, and Health Insurance: The Infant Health and Development Program," *American Journal of Public Health,* Vol. 84, No. 6, 1994, pp. 924–931.

Brown, Brett, Kristin Moore, and Sharon Bzostek, *A Portrait of Well-Being in Early Adulthood: A Report to the William and Flora Hewlett Foundation*, October 2003. Online at http://www. hewlett.org/ NR/rdonlyres/B0DB0AF1-02A4-455A-849A-AD582B767AF3AD582B 767AF3/0/FINALCOMPLETEPDFz.pdf (as of July 8, 2005).

Brown, Elizabeth G., and Catherine Scott-Little, *Evaluations of School Readiness Initiatives: What Are We Learning?* Greensboro, North Carolina: SERVE, March 2003. Online at http://www. serve.org/_downloads/REL/ELO/SchoolReadiness.pdf (as of July 12, 2005).

Burgess, Stephan R., Steven A. Hecht, and Christopher J. Lonigan, "Relationship of the Home Literacy Environment (HLE) to the Development of Reading-Related Abilities: A One-Year Longitudinal Study," *Reading Research Quarterly*, Vol. 37, No. 4, 2002, pp. 408–426.

Burtless, Gary, and Christopher Jencks, "American Inequality and Its Consequences," in Henry J. Aaron, James M. Lindsay and Pietro S. Nivola, eds., *Agenda for the Nation*, Washington, D.C.: Brookings Institution Press, 2003, pp. 61–108.

Business Roundtable and Corporate Voices for Working Families, *Early Childhood Education: A Call to Action from the Business Community*, Washington, D.C.: Business Roundtable, May 2003. Online at http:// www.brtable.org/pdf/901.pdf (as of February 22, 2005).

Campbell, Frances A., and Craig T. Ramey, "Effects of Early Intervention on Intellectual and Academic Achievement: A Follow-Up Study of Children from Low-Income Families," *Child Development*, Vol. 65, No. 2, 1994, pp. 684–698.

———, "Cognitive and School Outcomes for High-Risk African-American Students at Middle Adolescence: Positive Effects for Early Intervention," *American Educational Research Journal*, Vol. 32, No. 4, 1995, pp. 743–772.

Campbell, Frances A., Craig T. Ramey, Elizabeth Pungello, Joseph Sparling, and Shari Miller-Johnson, "Early Childhood Education: Young Adult Outcomes from the Abecedarian Project," *Applied Developmental Science*, Vol. 6, No. 1, 2002, pp. 42–57.

Carneiro, Pedro, and James J. Heckman, "Human Capital Policy," in James J. Heckman and Alan B. Krueger, eds., *Inequality in America: What Role for Human Capital Policies?* Cambridge, Mass.: MIT Press, 2003, pp. 77–239.

Child Trends, "Low and Very Low Birthweight Infants," *Child Trends DataBank*, Washington, D.C.: Child Trends, 2003. Online at http://www.childtrendsdatabank.org/indicators/57LowBirthweight.cfm (as of July 8, 2005).

Child Trends and Center for Child Health Research, *Early Child Development in Social Context: A Chartbook*, Publication No. 778, New York, N.Y.: The Commonwealth Fund, September 2004.

Cohen, Jacob, *Statistical Power Analysis for the Behavioral Sciences*, 2nd edition, Hillsdale, N.J.: Lawrence Erlbaum Associates, 1988.

Committee for Economic Development (CED), *Preschool for All: Investing in a Productive and Just Society*, New York, N.Y.: Committee for Economic Development, 2002. Online at http://www.ced.org/docs/report/report_preschool.pdf (as of July 8, 2005).

———, "Developmental Education: The Value of High Quality Preschool Investments as Economic Tools," CED Working Paper, September 2004. Online at http://www.ced.org/docs/report/report_preschool_2004_developmental.pdf (as of July 8, 2005).

Crane, Jonathan, *Social Programs That Work*, New York, N.Y.: Russell Sage Foundation, 1998.

Currie, Janet, "Early Childhood Education Programs," *Journal of Economic Perspectives*, Vol. 15, No. 2, 2001, pp. 213–238.

Currie, Janet and Matthew Neidell, "Getting Inside the 'Black Box' of Head Start Quality: What Matters and What Doesn't?" *Economics of Education Review*, forthcoming.

Currie, Janet, and Duncan Thomas, "Does Head Start Make a Difference?" *American Economic Review*, Vol. 85, No. 3, 1995, pp. 235–262.

———, "Does Head Start Help Hispanic Children?" *Journal of Public Economics*, Vol. 74, No. 2, 1999, pp. 235–262.

DeLong, J. Bradford, Claudia Goldin, and Lawrence F. Katz, "Sustaining U.S. Economic Growth," in Henry J. Aaron, James M. Lindsay, and Pietro S. Nivola, eds., *Agenda for the Nation*, Washington, D.C.: Brookings Institution Press, 2003, pp. 17–60.

Duncan, Greg J., and Jeanne Brooks-Gunn, eds., *Consequences of Growing Up Poor*, New York, N.Y.: Russell Sage Foundation, 1997.

Finn, Jeremy D., and Charles M. Achilles, "Tennessee's Class Size Study: Findings, Implications, Misconceptions," *Educational Evaluation and Policy Analysis*, Vol. 21, No. 2, 1999, pp. 97–110.

Garces, Eliana, Duncan Thomas, and Janet Currie, "Longer-Term Effects of Head Start," *American Economic Review*, Vol. 92, No. 4, 2002, pp. 999–1012.

Gilliam, Walter S., Carol H. Ripple, Edward F. Zigler, and Valerie Leiter, "Evaluating Child and Family Demonstration Initiatives: Lessons from the Comprehensive Child Development Program," *Early Childhood Research Quarterly*, Vol. 15, No. 1, 2000, pp. 41–59.

Golova, Natalia, Anthony J. Alario, Patrick M. Viver, Margarita Rodriguez, and Pamela C. High, "Literacy Promotion for Hispanic Families in a Primary Care Setting: A Randomized, Controlled Trial," *Pediatrics*, Vol. 103, No. 5, 1999, pp. 993–997.

Gomby, Deanna S., Patti L. Culross, and Richard E. Behrman, "Home Visiting: Recent Program Evaluations—Analysis and Recommendations," *The Future of Children*, Vol. 9, No. 1, 1999, pp. 4–26. Online at http://www.futureofchildren.org/usr_doc/vol9no1Art1.pdf (as of July 8, 2005).

Gormley, William T., and Ted Gayer, "Promoting School Readiness in Oklahoma: An Evaluation of Tulsa's Pre-K program," *Journal of Human Resources*, forthcoming.

Gormley, William T., Ted Gayer, Deborah Phillips, and Brittany Dawson, "The Effects of Universal Pre-K on Cognitive Development," *Developmental Psychology*, forthcoming.

Gray, Susan W., and Rupert A. Klaus, "The Early Training Project: A Seventh-Year Report," *Child Development*, Vol. 41, No. 4, 1970, pp. 909–924.

Gray, Susan W., and Barbara K. Ramsey, "The Early Training Project: A Life-Span View," *Human Development*, Vol. 25, No. 1, 1982, pp. 48–57.

Gray, Susan W., Barbara K. Ramsey, and Rupert A. Klaus, *From 3 to 20: The Early Training Project*, Baltimore, Md.: University Park Press, 1982.

————, "The Early Training Project: 1962–1980," in *As the Twig Is Bent: Lasting Effects of Preschool Programs*, The Consortium for Longitudinal Studies, Hillsdale, N.J.: Lawrence Erlbaum Associates, 1983, pp. 33–69.

Greenwood, Charles R., "Classwide Peer Tutoring: Longitudinal Effects on the Reading, Language, and Mathematics Achievement of At-Risk Students," *Journal of Reading, Writing and Learning Disabilities*, Vol. 7, No. 2, 1991, pp. 105–123.

Grigg, Wendy S., Mary C. Daane, Ying Jin, and Jay R. Campbell, *The Nation's Report Card: Reading 2002*, NCES 2003-521, Washington, D.C.: National Center for Education Statistics, U.S. Department of Education, 2003.

Hanushek, Eric A., and Dennis D. Kimko, "Schooling, Labor Force Quality, and the Growth of Nations," *American Economic Review*, Vol. 90, No. 5, 2000, pp. 1184–1208.

Haveman, Robert, and Barbara Wolfe, *Succeeding Generations: On the Effects of Investments in Children*, New York, N.Y.: Russell Sage Foundation, 1994.

————, "The Determinants of Children's Attainments: A Review of Methods and Findings," *Journal of Economic Literature*, Vol. XXXIII, 1995, pp. 1829–1878.

Hayes, Cheryl, John Palmer, and Martha Zaslow, *Who Cares for America's Children? Child Care Policy for the 1990s*, Washington, D.C.: The National Academy of Sciences Press, 1990.

Heckman, James J., "Policies to Foster Human Capital," *Research in Economics*, Vol. 54, No. 1, 2000, pp. 3–56.

Heckman, James J., and Dimitriy V. Masterov, "The Productivity Argument for Investing in Young Children," Working Paper 5, Invest in Kids Working Group, Washington, D.C.: Committee for Economic Development, October 2004.

Hedges, Larry V., "Distribution Theory for Glass's Estimator of Effect Size and Related Estimator," *Journal of Educational Statistics*, Vol. 6, 1981, pp. 107–128.

High, Pamela, Marita Hopmann, Linda LaGasse, and Holly Linn, "Evaluation of a Clinic-Based Program to Promote Book Sharing and Bedtime Routines Among Low-Income Urban Families with Young

Children," *Archives of Pediatrics and Adolescent Medicine*, Vol. 152, No. 5, 1998, pp. 459–465.

High, Pamela C., Linda LaGasse, Samuel Becker, Ingrid Ahlgren, and Adrian Gardner, "Literacy Promotion in Primary Care Pediatrics: Can We Make a Difference?" *Pediatrics*, Vol. 105, No. 4, 2000, pp. 927–934.

Hill, Jennifer L., Jeanne Brooks-Gunn, and Jane Waldfogel, "Sustained Effects of High Participation in an Early Intervention for Low-Birth-Weight Premature Infants," *Developmental Psychology*, Vol. 39, No. 4, 2003, pp. 730–744.

Honig, Alice Sterling, and J. Ronald Lally, "The Family Development Research Program: Retrospective Review," *Early Child Development and Care*, Vol. 10, 1982, pp. 41–62.

Huffman, Lynne C., Sarah L. Mehlinger, and Amy S. Kerivan, "Risk Factors for Academic and Behavioral Problems at the Beginning of School," in L. C. Huffman et al., *Off to a Good Start: Research on the Risk Factors for Early School Problems and Selected Federal Policies Affecting Children's Social and Emotional Development and Their Readiness for School*, Chapel Hill, N.C.: University of North Carolina, FPG Child Development Institute, 2001.

Infant Health and Development Project (IHDP), "Enhancing the Outcomes of Low-Birth-Weight, Premature Infants: A Multisite, Randomized Trial," *Journal of the American Medical Association*, Vol. 263, No. 22, 1990, p. 3035.

Johnson, Dale L., and James N. Breckenridge, "The Houston Parent-Child Development Center and the Primary Prevention of Behavior Problems in Young Children," *American Journal of Community Psychology*, Vol. 10, No. 3, 1982, pp. 305–316.

Johnson, Dale L., Hazel Leler, Laurel Rios, Larry Brandt, Alfred J. Kahn, Edward Mazeika, Martha Frede, and Billie Bisett, "The Houston Parent-Child Development Center: A Parent Education Program for Mexican-American Families," *American Journal of Orthopsychiatry*, Vol. 44, No. 1, 1974, pp. 121–128.

Johnson, Dale L., and Todd Walker, "A Follow-Up Evaluation of the Houston Parent-Child Development Center: School Performance," *Journal of Early Intervention*, Vol. 15, 1991, pp. 226–236.

Karoly, Lynn A., and James H. Bigelow, *The Economics of Investing in Universal Preschool Education in California*, Santa Monica, Calif.: The RAND Corporation, MG-349-PF, 2005.

Karoly, Lynn A., Peter W. Greenwood, Susan S. Everingham, Jill Houbé, M. Rebecca Kilburn, C. Peter Rydell, Matthew Sanders, and James Chiesa, *Investing in Our Children: What We Know and Don't Know About the Costs and Benefits of Early Childhood Interventions*, Santa Monica, Calif.: RAND Corporation, MR-898-TCWF, 1998.

Karoly, Lynn A., M. Rebecca Kilburn, James H. Bigelow, Jonathan P. Caulkins, and Jill Cannon, *Assessing Costs and Benefits of Early Childhood Intervention Programs: Overview and Application to the Starting Early Starting Smart Program*, Santa Monica, Calif.: RAND Corporation, MR-1336-CFP, 2001.

Karoly, Lynn A., and Constantijn W.A. Panis, *The 21st Century at Work: Forces Shaping the Future Workforce and Workplace in the United States*, Santa Monica, Calif.: RAND Corporation, MG-164-DOL, 2004.

Krueger, Alan B., and Mikael Lindahl, "Education for Growth: Why and for Whom?" *Journal of Economic Literature*, Vol. 39, No. 4, 2001, pp. 1101–1136.

Lally, J. Ronald, Peter L. Mangione, and Alice S. Honig, "The Syracuse University Family Development Research Program: Long-Range Impact of an Early Intervention with Low-Income Children and Their Families," in *Parent Educaton as Early Childhood Intervention: Emerging Directions in Theory, Research and Practice,* D. R. Powell and I. E. Sigel, eds., Norwood, N.J.: Ablex Publishing Corporation, 1988.

Landry, Susan H., *Effective Early Childhood Programs: Turning Knowledge into Action*, Houston, Texas: University of Texas Health Science Center at Houston, 2005.

Lazar, Irving, and Richard Darlington, "Lasting Effects of Early Education: A Report from the Consortium for Longitudinal Studies," *Monographs of the Society for Research in Child Development*, Vol. 47(2–4), Serial No. 195, 1982.

Lipsey, Mark W., and David Wilson, *Practical Meta-Analysis*, Thousand Oaks, Calif.: Sage Publications, 2001.

Lochner, Lance, and Enrico Moretti, "The Effect of Education on Crime: Evidence from Prison Inmates, Arrests, and Self-Reports," *American Economic Review*, Vol. 94, No. 1, January 2004, pp. 155–189.

Love, John M., Ellen E. Kisker, Christine M. Ross, Peter Z. Schochet, Jeanne Brooks-Gunn, Diane Paulsell, Kimberly Boller, Jill Constantine, Cheri Vogel, Allison Sidle Fuligni, and Christy Brady-Smith, *Making a Difference in the Lives of Infants and Toddlers and Their Families: The Impacts of Early Head Start. Executive Summary,* Washington, D.C.: Administration on Children, Youth, and Families, U.S. Department of Health and Human Services, 2002a.

———, *Making a Difference in the Lives of Infants and Toddlers and Their Families: The Impacts of Early Head Start*, Vol. I, *Final Technical Report*, Washington, D.C.: Administration on Children, Youth, and Families, U.S. Department of Health and Human Services, 2002b.

Love, John M., Peter Z. Schochet, and Alicia L. Meckstroth, *Are They in Any Real Danger? What Research Does—and Doesn't—Tell Us About Child Care Quality and Children's Well-Being*, Princeton, N.J.: Mathematica Policy Research, Inc., May 1996.

Masse, Leonard N., and W. Steven Barnett, "A Benefit-Cost Analysis of the Abecedarian Early Childhood Intervention," in Henry M. Levin and Patrick J. McEwan, eds., *Cost-Effectiveness and Educational Policy*, Larchmont, N.Y.: Eye on Education, Inc., 2002, pp. 157–173.

Mayer, Susan E., *What Money Can't Buy: Family Income and Children's Life Chances*, Cambridge, Mass.: Harvard University Press, 1997.

McCarton, Cecelia M., Jeanne Brooks-Gunn, Ina F. Wallace, Charles R. Bauer, Forrest C. Bennett, Judy C. Bernbaum, Sue Broyles, Patrick H. Casey, Marie C. McCormick, David T. Scott, Jon Tyson, James Tonascia, and Curtis L. Meinert, "Results at Age 8 Years of Early Intervention for Low-Birth-Weight Premature Infants," *Journal of the American Medical Association*, Vol. 277, No. 2, 1997, pp. 126–132.

McCormick, Marie C., Jeanne Brooks-Gunn, Sam Shapiro, April A. Benasich, George Black, and Ruth T. Gross, "Health Care Use Among Young Children in Day Care: Results in a Randomized Trial of Early Intervention," *Journal of the American Medical Association*, Vol. 265, No. 17, 1991, pp. 2212–2217.

McCormick, Marie C., Cecelia M. McCarton, James Tonascia, and Jeanne Brooks-Gunn, "Early Educational Intervention for Very Low Birth Weight Infants: Results from the Infant Health and Development Program," *Journal of Pediatrics*, Vol. 123, 1993, pp. 527–533.

Meisels, Samuel J., and Jack P. Shonkoff, "Early Childhood Intervention: A Continuing Evolution," in Jack P. Shonkoff and Samuel J. Meisels, eds., *Handbook of Early Childhood Intervention*, 2nd edition, New York, N.Y.: Cambridge University Press, 2000, pp. 3–31.

Miller, Ted R., Mark A. Cohen, and Brian Wiersema, *Victim Costs and Consequences: A New Look*, Washington, D.C.: National Institute of Justice, January 1996.

Miller-Heyl, Jan, David MacPhee, and Janet J. Fritz, "DARE to be You: A Family-Support, Early Prevention Program," *Journal of Primary Prevention*, Vol. 18, No. 3, 1998, pp. 257–285.

Minkovitz, Cynthia S., Nancy Hughart, Donna Strobino, Dan Scharfstein, Holly Grason, William Hou, Tess Miller, David Bishai, Marilyn Augustyn, Kathryn Taaffe McLearn, and Bernard Guyer, "A Practice-Based Intervention to Enhance the Quality of Care in the First 3 Years of Life," *Journal of the American Medical Association*, Vol. 290, 2003, pp. 3081–3091.

Neckerman, Kathryn M., *Social Inequality*, New York: Russell Sage Foundation, 2004.

Nelson, Charles A., "The Neurobiological Bases of Early Intervention," in Jack P. Shonkoff and Samuel J. Meisels, eds., *Handbook of Early Childhood Intervention*, 2nd edition, New York: Cambridge University Press, 2000, pp. 41–59.

Nelson, Geoffrey, Anne Westhues, and Jennifer MacLeod, "A Meta-Analysis of Longitudinal Research on Preschool Prevention Programs for Children," *Prevention & Treatment*, Vol. 6, Article 31, December 18, 2003. Online at http://journals.apa.org/prevention/volume6/pre0060031a.html (as of July 8, 2005).

Olds, David L., *Reducing Risks for Childhood-Onset Conduct Disorder with Prenatal and Early Childhood Home Visitation*, American Public Health Association Pre-Conference Workshop, New York, N.Y., 1996.

Olds, David L., John Eckenrode, Charles R. Henderson, Jr., Harriet Kitzman, Jane Powers, Robert Cole, Kimberly Sidora, Pamela Morris,

Lisa M. Pettitt, and Dennis Luckey, "Long-Term Effects of Home Visitation on Maternal Life Course and Child Abuse and Neglect: Fifteen-Year Follow-Up of a Randomized Trial," *Journal of the American Medical Association*, Vol. 278, No. 8, 1997, pp. 637–643.

Olds, David L., Charles R. Henderson, Jr., Robert Chamberlin, and Robert Tatelbaum, "Preventing Child Abuse and Neglect: A Randomized Trial of Nurse Home Visitation," *Pediatrics*, Vol. 78, No. 1, 1986, pp. 65–78.

Olds, David L., Charles R. Henderson, Jr., and Harriet Kitzman, "Does Prenatal and Infancy Nurse Home Visitation Have Enduring Effects on Qualities of Parental Caregiving and Child Health at 25 to 50 Months of Life?" *Pediatrics*, Vol. 93, No. 1, 1994, pp. 82–88.

Olds, David L., Charles R. Henderson, Jr., Robert Tatelbaum, and Robert Chamberlin, "Improving the Delivery of Prenatal Care and Outcomes of Pregnancy: A Randomized Trial of Nurse Home Visitation," *Pediatrics*, Vol. 77, No. 1, 1986, pp. 16–28.

————, "Improving the Life-Course Development of Socially Disadvantaged Mothers: A Randomized Trial of Nurse Home Visitation," *American Journal of Public Health*, Vol. 78, No. 11, 1988, pp. 1436–1445.

Olds, David, Harriet Kitzman, Robert Cole, and JoAnn Robinson, "Theoretical Foundations of a Program of Home Visitation for Pregnant Women and Parents of Young Children," *Journal of Community Psychology*, Vol. 25, No. 1, 1997, pp. 9–25.

Olds, David L., Harriet Kitzman, Robert Cole, JoAnn Robinson, Kimberly Sidora, Dennis W. Luckey, Charles R. Henderson, Jr., Carole Hanks, Jessica Bondy, and John Holmberg, "Effects of Nurse Home-Visiting on Maternal Life Course and Child Development: Age 6 Follow-Up Results of a Randomized Trial," *Pediatrics*, Vol. 114, No. 6, 2004, pp. 1550–1559.

Olds, David L., JoAnn Robinson, Ruth O'Brien, Dennis W. Luckey, Lisa M. Pettit, Charles R. Henderson, Jr., Rosanna K. Ng, Karen L. Sheff, Jon Korfmacher, Susan Hiatt, and Ayelet Tahmi, "Home Visiting by Paraprofessionals and by Nurses: A Randomized, Controlled Trial," *Pediatrics*, Vol. 110, No. 3, 2002, pp. 486–496.

Olds, David L., JoAnn Robinson, Lisa Pettitt, Dennis W. Luckey, John Holmberg, Rosanna K. Ng, Kathy Isacks, Karen Sheff, and Charles R.

Henderson, Jr., "Effects of Home Visits by Paraprofessionals and by Nurses: Age 4 Follow-Up Results of a Randomized Trial," *Pediatrics*, Vol. 114, No. 6, 2004, pp. 1560–1568.

Perloff, Linda, Pamela Butler, Carolyn Berry, and Peter Budetti, "Literature Review of Outcomes of Early Intervention Programs," Evanston, Ill.: Institute for Health Services Research and Policy Studies, Northwestern University, August 1998. Online at http://www.northwestern.edu/ihsrps/research/review.PDF (as of July 8, 2005)

Peters, Alan H., and Peter S. Fisher, *State Enterprise Zone Programs: Have They Worked?* Kalamazoo, Mich.: The W. E. Upjohn Institute for Employment Research, 2002.

Ramey, Craig T., Donna M. Bryant, Joseph J. Sparling, and Barbara H. Wasik, "Project CARE: A Comparison of Two Early Intervention Strategies to Prevent Retarded Development," *Topics in Early Childhood Special Education*, Vol. 5, No. 2, 1985, pp. 12–25.

Ramey, Craig T., Donna M. Bryant, Barbara H. Wasik, Joseph J. Sparling, Kaye H. Fendt, and Lisa M. La Vange, "Infant Health and Development Program for Low Birth Weight, Premature Infants: Program Elements, Family Participation, and Child Intelligence," *Pediatrics*, Vol. 89, No. 3, 1992, pp. 454–465.

Ramey, Craig T., and Frances A. Campbell, "Preventive Education for High-Risk Children: Cognitive Consequences of the Carolina Abecedarian Project," *American Journal of Mental Deficiency*, Vol. 88, No. 5, 1984, pp. 515–523.

———, "Poverty, Early Childhood Education, and Academic Competence: The Abecedarian Experiment," in Aletha Huston, ed., *Children Reared in Poverty*, New York, N.Y.: Cambridge University Press, 1994, pp. 190–221.

Ramey, Craig T., and Sharon L. Ramey, "Early Learning and School Readiness: Can Early Intervention Make a Difference?" *Merrill-Palmer Quarterly*, Vol. 50, No. 4, 2004, pp. 471–491.

Rathburn, Amy, Jerry West, and Elvira Germino-Hausken, *From Kindergarten Through Third Grade: Children's Beginning School Experiences*, NCES 2004-007, Washington, D.C.: U.S. Government Printing Office, 2004.

Resnick, Michael B., Fonda D. Eyler, Robert M. Nelson, Donald V. Eitzman, and Richard L. Buciarelli, "Developmental Intervention for Low Birth Weight Infants: Improved Early Developmental Outcome," *Pediatrics*, Vol. 80, No. 1, 1987, pp. 68–74.

Reynolds, Arthur J., "Effects of a Preschool Plus Follow-On Intervention for Children at Risk," *Developmental Psychology*, Vol. 30, No. 6, 1994, pp. 787–804.

———, "One Year of Preschool Intervention or Two: Does It Matter?" *Early Childhood Research Quarterly*, Vol. 10, 1995, pp. 1–31.

———, *The Chicago Child-Parent Centers: A Longitudinal Study of Extended Early Childhood Intervention*, Madison, Wisc.: University of Wisconsin–Madison, March 1997.

———, *Success in Early Intervention: The Chicago Child-Parent Centers*, Lincoln, Neb.: University of Nebraska Press, 2000.

Reynolds, Arthur J., H. Chang, and Judy A. Temple, *Early Educational Intervention and Juvenile Delinquency: Findings from the Chicago Longitudinal Studies*, paper presented at the SRCD Seminar on Early Intervention Effects on Delinquency and Crime, Washington, D.C., April 1997.

Reynolds, Arthur J., and Judy A. Temple, "Quasi-Experimental Estimates of the Effects of a Preschool Intervention," *Evaluation Review*, Vol. 19, No. 4, 1995, pp. 347–373.

———, "Extended Early Childhood Intervention and School Achievement: Age Thirteen Findings from the Chicago Longitudinal Study," *Child Development*, Vol. 69, 1998, pp. 231–246.

Reynolds, Arthur J., Judy A. Temple, Dylan L. Robertson, and Emily A. Mann, "Long-Term Effects of an Early Childhood Intervention on Educational Achievement and Juvenile Arrest: A 15-Year Follow-Up of Low-Income Children in Public Schools," *Journal of the American Medical Association*, Vol. 285, No. 18, May 9, 2001, pp. 2339–2346.

———, "Age 21 Cost-Benefit Analysis of the Title I Chicago Child-Parent Centers," *Educational Evaluation and Policy Analysis*, Vol. 24, No. 4, Winter 2002, pp. 267–303.

Roggman, Lori A., Lisa K. Boyce, Gina A. Cook, and Andrea D. Hart, *Making a Difference in the Lives of Infants and Toddlers and Their*

Families: The Impacts of Early Head Start, Volume III: *Local Contributions to Understanding the Programs and Their Impacts,* Washington, D.C.: Administration on Children, Youth, and Families, U.S. Department of Health and Human Services, 2002. Online at www.mathinc.com/publications/PDFs/ehsfinalvol3.pdf (as of July 12, 2005).

Rolnick, Art, and Rob Grunewald, "Early Childhood Development: Economic Development with a High Public Return," *fedgazette,* March 2003. Online at http://minneapolisfed.org/pubs/fedgaz/03-03/earlychild.cfm (as of July 8, 2005).

Ruopp, Richard, Jeffrey Travers, Frederic Glantz, and C. Coelen, *Children at the Center: Final Report of the National Day Care Study,* Cambridge, Mass.: Abt Associates, ED 168 733, 1979.

St. Pierre, Robert G., Jean. I. Layzer, and Helen V. Barnes, "Two-Generation Programs: Design, Cost, and Short-Term Effectiveness," *The Future of Children,* Vol. 5, Winter 1995, pp. 76–93.

St. Pierre, Robert G., Jean I. Layzer, Barbara D. Goodson, and Lawrence S. Bernstein, *National Impact Evaluation of the Comprehensive Child Development Program,* Cambridge, Mass.: Abt Associates, 1997. Online at http://www.abtassoc.com/reports/D19970050.pdf (as of July 8, 2005).

Sameroff, Arnold J., and Michael J. Chandler, "Reproductive Risk and the Continuum of Caretaking Causalty," in Frances D. Horowitz et al., eds., *Review of Child Development Research,* Volume 4, Chicago, Ill.: University of Chicago Press, 1975.

Sanders, Lee M., Tamar D. Gershon, Lynne C. Huffman, and Fernando S. Mendoza, "Prescribing Books for Immigrant Children,"*Archives of Pediatrics and Adolescent Medicine,* Vol. 154, No. 8, 2000, pp. 771–777.

Schweinhart, Lawrence J., *The High/Scope Perry Preschool Study Through Age 40: Summary, Conclusions, and Frequently Asked Questions,* Ypsilanti, Mich.: High/Scope Educational Research Foundation, 2004.

Schweinhart, Lawrence J., Helen V. Barnes, and David P. Weikart, *Significant Benefits: The High/Scope Perry Preschool Study Through Age 27,* Monographs of the High/Scope Educational Research Foundation, 10, Ypsilanti, Mich.: High/Scope Press, 1993.

Schweinhart, Lawrence J., Jeanne Montie, Zongping Xiang, W. Steven Barnett, Clive R. Belfield, and Milagros Nores, *Lifetime Effects: The High/Scope Perry Preschool Study Through Age 40*, Monographs of the High/Scope Educational Research Foundation, 14, Ypsilanti, Mich.: High/Scope Press, 2005.

Schweinhart, Lawrence J., and David P. Weikart, *Young Children Grow Up: The Effects of the Perry Preschool Program on Youths Through Age 15*, Monographs of the High/Scope Educational Research Foundation, 7, Ypsilanti, Mich.: High/Scope Press, 1980.

Schweke, William, *Smart Money: Education and Economic Development*, Washington, D.C.: Economic Policy Institute, 2004.

Shadish, William R., Thomas D. Cook, and Donald T. Campbell, *Experimental and Quasi-Experimental Designs for Generalized Causal Inference*, Boston, Mass.: Houghton Mifflin Company, 2001.

Shonkoff, Jack P., and Deborah A. Phillips, eds., *From Neurons to Neighborhoods: The Science of Early Child Development*, Washington, D.C.: National Academy Press, 2000.

Shore, Rima, *Rethinking the Brain: New Insights into Early Development*, New York: Families and Work Institute, 1997.

Snow, Catherine E., M. Susan Burns, and Peg Griffin, eds., *Preventing Reading Difficulties in Young Children*, Washington, D.C.: National Academy Press, 1998.

Strickland, Dorothy S., and W. Steven Barnett, "Literacy Interventions for Preschool Children Considered At Risk: Implications for Curriculum, Professional Development, and Parent Involvement," in Colleen M. Fairbanks, Jo Worthy, Beth Maloch, James V. Hoffman, and Diane L. Schallert, eds., *52nd Yearbook of the National Reading Conference*, Oak Creek, Wisc.: National Reading Conference, Inc., 2004, pp. 104–116.

Sweet, Monica A., and Mark I. Appelbaum, "Is Home Visiting an Effective Strategy? A Meta-Analytic Review of Home Visiting Programs for Families with Young Children," *Child Development*, Vol. 75, No. 5, September/October 2004, pp. 1435–1456.

U.S. Census Bureau, *School Enrollment—Social and Economic Characteristics of Students*, Washington, D.C.: U.S. Census Bureau, undated. Online at http://www.census.gov/population/www/socdemo/school.html (as of February 22, 2005).

U.S. Department of Education, National Center for Education Statistics, *Dropout Rates in the United States: 1995*, NCES 97-473, Washington, D.C.: U.S. Department of Education, July 1997.

U.S. Department of Education, National Center for Education Statistics, *The Condition of Education 2003*, NCES 2003-067, Washington, D.C.: U.S. Government Printing Office, 2003.

U.S. Department of Education, National Center for Education Statistics, *The Nation's Report Card: Mathematics Highlights 2003*, NCES 2004-451, Washington, D.C.: U.S. Department of Education, 2004a.

U.S. Department of Education, National Center for Education Statistics, *The Nation's Report Card: Reading Highlights 2003*, NCES 2004-452, Washington, D.C.: U.S. Department of Education, 2004b.

U.S. Department of Health and Human Services, Administration for Children and Families, *Head Start Impact Study, 2000–2006*, Washington, D.C.: Administration for Children and Families, last updated April 19, 2005. Online at http://www.acf.hhs.gov/programs/opre/hs/impact_study/index.html (as of July 8, 2005).

U.S. Department of Labor, Bureau of Labor Statistics, *Consumer Price Index—All Urban Consumers (CPI-U)*, Washington, D.C.: U.S. Department of Labor, undated. Online at http://data.bls.gov/cgi-bin/surveymost?cu (as of January 14, 2005).

Vandell, Deborah Lowe, and Barbara Wolfe, *Child Care Quality: Does It Matter and Does It Need to Be Improved?* Washington, D.C.: U.S. Department of Health and Human Services, May 2000. Online at http://aspe.hhs.gov/hsp/ccquality00/index.htm (as of July 8, 2005).

Vandivere, Sharon, Lindsay Pitzer, Tamara G. Halle, and Elizabeth C. Hair, "Indicators of Early School Success and Child Well-Being," *Cross Currents*, Issue 3, October 2004. Online at http://www.childtrendsdatabank.org (as of July 8, 2005).

Viscusi, W. Kip, Wesley A. Magat, and Anne Forrest, "Altruistic and Private Valuations of Risk Reduction," *Journal of Policy Analysis and Management*, Vol. 7, No. 2, Winter 1988, pp. 227–245.

Wagner, Mary M., Renee Cameto, and Suzanne Gerlach-Downie, *Intervention in Support of Adolescent Parents and Their Children: A Final Report on the Teen Parents as Teachers Demonstration*, Menlo Park, Calif.: SRI International, 1996.

Wagner, Mary M., and Serena L. Clayton, "The Parents as Teachers Program: Results from Two Demonstrations," *The Future of the Children*, Vol. 9, No. 1, 1999, pp. 91–115.

Wagner, Mary, Serena Clayton, Suzanne Gerlach-Downie, and Mark McElroy. *An Evaluation of the Northern California Parents as Teachers Demonstration*, Menlo Park, Calif.: SRI International, 1999.

Wagner, Mary, Elizabeth Iida, Donna Spiker, Frances Hernandez, and Julia Song, *The Multisite Evaluation of the Parents as Teachers Home Visiting Program: Three-Year Findings from One Community*, Menlo Park, Calif.: SRI International, 2001.

Wagner, Mary, Camille Marder, and Jose Blackorby, *The Children We Serve: The Demographic Characteristics of Elementary and Middle School Students with Disabilities and Their Households*, Menlo Park, Calif.: SRI International, September 2002.

Wagner, Mary, Donna Spiker, Frances Hernandez, Julia Song, and Suzanne Gerlach-Downie, *Multisite Parents as Teachers Evaluation: Experiences and Outcomes for Children and Families*, Menlo Park, Calif.: SRI International, 2001.

Wasik, Barbara Hanna, Craig T. Ramey, Donna M. Bryant, and Joseph J. Sparling, "A Longitudinal Study of Two Early Intervention Strategies: Project CARE," *Child Development*, Vol. 61, No. 6, 1990, pp. 1682–1696.

Webster-Stratton, Carolyn, "Preventing Conduct Problems in Head Start Children: Strengthening Parent Competencies," *Journal of Consulting and Clinical Psychology*, Vol. 66, No. 5, 1998, pp. 715–730.

Webster-Stratton, Carolyn, Mary Kolpacoff, and Terri Hollinsowth, "Self-Administered Videotape Therapy for Families with Conduct-Problem Children: Comparison with Two Cost-Effective Treatments and a Control Group," *Journal of Consulting and Clinical Psychology*, Vol. 56, No. 4, 1988, pp. 558–566.

Webster-Stratton, Carolyn, Jamila Reid, and Mary Hammond, "Preventing Conduct Problems in Head Start Children: A Parent and Teacher Training Partnership in Head Start," *Journal of Clinical Child Psychology*, Vol. 30, No. 3, 2001, pp. 283–302.

Weikart, David P., J. T. Bond, and J. T. McNeil, *The Ypsilanti Perry Preschool Project: Preschool Years and Longitudinal Results Through*

Fourth Grade, Monographs of the High/Scope Educational Research Foundation, 3, Ypsilanti, Mich.: High/Scope Press, 1978.

West, Jerry, Kristin Denton, and Elvira Germino-Hausken, *America's Kindergartners*, NCES 2000-070, Washington, D.C.: U.S. Government Printing Office, 2000.

Whitehurst, Grover J., and Christopher J. Lonigan, "Child Development and Emergent Literacy," *Child Development*, Vol. 69, No. 3, 1998, pp. 848–872.

Wirt, John, Susan Choy, Patrick Rooney, Stephen Provasnik, Anindita Sen, and Richard Tobin, *The Condition of Education 2004*, NCES 2004-077, Washington, D.C.: U.S. Government Printing Office, 2004.

Wolfe, Barbara L., and Robert H. Haveman, "Social and Nonmarket Benefits form Education in an Advanced Economy," in Yolanda K. Kodrzycki, ed., *Education in the 21st Century: Meeting the Challenges of a Changing World*, Conference Series No. 47, Boston, Mass.: Federal Reserve Bank of Boston, 2002, pp. 97–131.

Yoshikawa, Hirokazu, "Long-Term Effects of Early Childhood Programs on Social Outcomes and Delinquency," *The Future of Children*, Vol. 5, 1995, pp. 51–75.

Zill, Nicholas, and Jerry West, *Entering Kindergarten: A Portrait of American Children When They Begin School*, NCES 2001-035, Washington, D.C.: U.S. Government Printing Office, 2001.

Zuckerman, Barry, Steven Parker, Margot Kaplan-Sanoff, Marilyn Augustyn, and Michael C. Barth, "Healthy Steps: A Case Study of Innovation in Pediatric Practice," *Pediatrics*, Vol. 114, 2004, pp. 820–826.